THE INLAND STEEL FLEET

1911-1998

LARGE PRINT EDITION

By Raymond A. Bawal, Jr.

INLAND

EXPRESSIONS

Clinton Township, Michigan

Published by Inland Expressions

Inland Expressions
42211 Garfield Rd. #297
Clinton Township, MI. 48038

www.inlandexpressions.com

Large Print Edition 2016

The text of this large print book is unabridged, but some aspects may differ from the original edition.

ISBN-13 978-1-939150-15-8

Design by Inland Expressions

Front Cover: The *Edward L. Ryerson* steams downbound on the picturesque St. Marys River in June of 1997. (Author's Collection)

TABLE OF CONTENTS

Preface

Although a single volume, this book is divided into two distinct sections to provide the reader with a convenient method to explore the history of the Inland Steel fleet and that of each individual vessel operated by the steelmaker between 1911 and 1998. The first section of this book chronicles the history of this fleet from its inception to its demise following Ispat International's purchase of the Inland Steel Company in 1998. In order to provide a detailed and complete history of each vessel that sailed under Inland Steel colors throughout this timeframe, the second section not only relates significant events taking place during its time in the fleet, but, when necessary, also prior and subsequent operations for other shipping firms. As such, some duplication of certain details between each section is unavoidable despite best efforts to minimize such redundancies. Such a format, however, affords the reader the opportunity to explore a particular vessel's history without having to search for details within the fleet history section.

It is interesting to note that some eighteen years following the sale of the Inland Steel Company to a foreign steel corporation, the three ships owned by the steelmaker at the time survive today as fleet mates in the

Central Marine Logistics fleet. While only two remain currently active (a third is in long-term layup), these ships continue to operate upon long established trade routes dedicated to supplying the former Inland Steel mill at Indiana Harbor, Indiana with the raw materials necessary for the production of steel. Although some minor changes have occurred over the years, for the most part these vessels retain the former fleet colors that made the Inland Steel fleet one of the most recognizable shipping firms to have ever operated on the Great Lakes.

All of the photographs appearing in this publication come from my personal collection obtained over a span of time stretching nearly thirty years in length. In cases in which a particular photographer has signed his work, I have provided credit at the end of caption accompanying each image. Unfortunately, several of the photographs included in this book contain no signature marks, thus their creators remain unknown.

It is hoped that this publication will allow the reader to gain a new insight into the history of the Inland Steel fleet and the ships that sailed in its service.

Introduction

Looking down from space in the darkness of night one of the most prominent features on the continent of North America is the outline of southern Lake Michigan. Hidden among the glow created by the concentration of heavy industry some twenty miles southeast of downtown Chicago is Indiana Harbor, Indiana. Along the shore of this manmade harbor, the Inland Steel Company began operating a steel mill in 1902 that in time was destined to grow into one of the largest steel works in the nation.

In 1893, an estimated 28 million people descended upon Chicago to attend the World's Fair. Among these visitors was an iron merchant from Cincinnati, Ohio named Joseph Block and his 22-year old son, Philip D. Block. During their time in the city, a local group approached the two men with a proposal to establish a new enterprise from the remnants of a defunct steel company that failed to survive the financial panic gripping the nation that year. Sensing opportunity during a time of economic uncertainty, the Blocks along with six other investors founded the Inland Steel Company at Chicago Heights in October of 1893. Just after the turn of the century, the growing company entered a new chapter in its history by building a new open-hearth mill at Indiana Harbor.

Selling a majority of its products to customers within 500 miles of the Chicago area, Indiana Harbor provided the Inland Steel Company with a perfect location in which to operate its steel works. The site also facilitated the efficient bulk delivery of iron ore, coal, and limestone, the three necessary ingredients for the manufacture of steel, by freighters plying the waters of the Great Lakes. Growing quickly during a time in which the United States emerged as the world's mightiest industrialized nation, the steelmaker stood ready to make its first foray into vessel ownership just eighteen years following its founding.

Part One

Fleet History

Chapter One
The Early Years 1911-1935

Merging its various fleets into the Acme Transit Company during the last half of 1911, the Hawgood family found it necessary to sell four of its vessels to cover outstanding debts associated with its shipping concerns. Presented with an opportunity to acquire relatively new vessels at a reasonable cost, the Inland Steel Company engaged Hutchinson & Company of Cleveland, Ohio to act as its agent to purchase the steamers *Arthur H. Hawgood* and *W. R. Woodford*. Financial troubles experienced by the Hawgood organization combined with a depressed market for ships placed the steelmaker in a favorable position to begin its own fleet to transport raw materials into its manufacturing facility at Indiana Harbor, Indiana. Following the beginning of negotiations in June of that year, both steamers underwent a survey by Babcock & Penton, naval engineers and architects, before the Inland Steel Company completed the purchase agreement on September 1, 1911.

Products of the American Ship Building Company, the construction of these steamers had taken place at that firm's West Bay City Shipbuilding Company division at

West Bay City, Michigan. Built in 1907, the *Arthur H. Hawgood* measured 569 feet in length while the *W. R. Woodford*, launched the following year, had a slightly shorter length of 552 feet. In keeping with vessel ownership practices of the time to limit liability in the event of a major accident, the Hawgood family had created a number of individual fleets to operate its overall holdings. As such, the *Hawgood* and *Woodford* entered service for the Neptune Steamship Company and the Hawgood Transportation Company respectively.

Following their acquisition, the Inland Steel Company placed these two vessels into a newly created joint venture between that firm and Hutchinson & Company named the Inland Steamship Company. As the majority shareholder, the steelmaker owned a 67 ½ percent stake in this enterprise with the remaining 32 ½ percent of the shares being held by Hutchinson & Company. At the same time, Inland Steel also entered into a management agreement with Hutchinson to operate its two vessels. Although unknown to either firm at the time, this arrangement was to last for forty-five years.

In a pair of letters dated December 23, 1911, the U.S. Department of Commerce and Labor endorsed a request by the Inland Steamship Company to rename the *Arthur H. Hawgood* to *Joseph Block* and the *W. R. Woodford* to *N. F. Leopold*. Entered into the calendar for the second session of the 62d Congress on January 29 of the following year as bills S.3869 & S.3870, approval for this change came quickly with both vessels receiving their new names prior to the beginning of the 1912 shipping season. With a combined single trip carrying capacity of 21,000 gross tons, the two ships of the Inland Steamship Company were among the giants of their day. Although purchased by Inland Steel to transport raw materials into its steel plant at Indiana Harbor, the management agreement with Hutchinson & Company resulted in the *Joseph Block* and *N. F. Leopold* frequently carrying cargoes outside of their owner's direct requirements.

The steamer *Joseph Block* while operating for the Inland Steamship Company. (Author's Collection)

The origin of the Inland Steel Company can be traced back to the Panic of 1893 when a financial collapse resulted in a large number of companies going out of business. One such firm that failed to survive the economic recession was the Chicago Steel Works when it went into receivership in September of that year. With the production equipment saved by Ross Buckingham, a brother of the steel company's former president, a small group of investors led by Joseph Block and his son, Philip D. Block, formed the Inland Steel Company at Chicago Heights, Illinois on October 30, 1893. Though the newly formed company struggled through its first year of existence, it nonetheless brought in enough income in 1894 to pay its shareholders a dividend.

In 1901, Inland Steel accepted a proposal from a land developer involving a 50-acre parcel of land bordering Lake Michigan offered for sale to any company willing to build a new steel plant on the site. Located within easy access to existing rail lines and waterborne transportation, the property was to become the site of Inland's Indiana Harbor plant. Having first placed its new steel plant into operation in 1902, the company progressively expanded the facility throughout the balance of the decade despite experiencing several years of financial hardship. The year of 1906 proved especially significant to Inland Steel as it completed construction of the first blast furnace to enter operation in northern Indiana.

Situated at the southern end of Lake Michigan some twenty miles from downtown Chicago, the location of Indiana Harbor makes it ideally suited to receive deliveries of iron ore, coal, and limestone—the three basic raw materials required for the production of steel—from lake freighters plying the waters of the Great Lakes. This allowed Inland Steel to capitalize upon a dependable and economical method to receive its raw materials, thus increasing both the efficiency and profitability of its steel making operation.

In 1906, Inland Steel purchased the Laura Iron Mine located near Hibbing, Minnesota. This acquisition provided the steelmaker with a dedicated source for its most important raw material while also significantly reducing its overall costs. The process towards a vertical integration of its operations was to lead directly to the formation of the Inland Steamship Company five years later.

During the latter days of the Inland Steamship Company's second full season of operation, the Great Lakes experienced the most devastating storm in its recorded history. Wreaking havoc as it swept across the region during November 7-10, 1913, this weather system led to the sinking of twelve vessels with their entire crews. Significant among these losses were eight steel steamers no more than ten years old, including one, the 556-foot long *James Carruthers*, which had entered service earlier that year. In addition, six other ships were so severely damaged that their owners abandoned them as total constructive losses. While an exact death toll is impossible to determine, the storm caused at least 235 fatalities among the crews aboard the vessels caught in the tempest.

While Lake Huron suffered the most heavily in terms of marine destruction with eight steamers sunk and another seven damaged to various degrees ranging from minor to severe, only Lake Ontario escaped the storm without any vessel losses. Despite leaving its mark across all five of the Great Lakes, the Inland Steamship Company's *N. F. Leopold* and *Joseph Block* sustained no damage during the Great Lakes Storm of 1913.

One of two ships lost in Lake Superior during the storm was the 545-foot long *Henry B. Smith*. A former fleet mate to Inland Steamship's two steamers while they were members of the Hawgood fleet, this ship began its final voyage when it departed Marquette, Michigan at 5 p.m. on November 9, 1913 with a load of iron ore destined for delivery to a lower Great Lakes port. Operated by Hawgood's Acme Transit Company, the *Smith* encountered trouble a short time later and sank with the loss of its twenty-five crewmembers. Destined to remain hidden for nearly one-hundred years in the dark depths of Lake Superior, the wreck of the *Henry B. Smith* was finally discovered during the spring of 2013 resting in 535 feet of water.

Not limiting its destruction to marine traffic, the heavy winds and blinding snow generated by the 1913 Storm caused considerable damage to several of the communities surrounding the lakes. Although its ships escaped unscathed, blizzard conditions knocked out the blast furnaces at Inland Steel's mill at Indiana Harbor on November 9, 1913 even as heavy waves seriously damaged that port's breakwater. Although the storm had abated in the Chicago area by the late hours of the following day, Indiana Harbor became the scene of further devastation when the explosion of a steam pipe at Inland Steel killed three workers.

Having increased its steel making capabilities steadily since its 1893 founding, the onset of World War I in 1914 fueled Inland Steel's continued growth, the capacity of which reached 1 million tons for the first time in 1917. That same year, lake freighters moved 62,498,901 gross tons of iron ore across the Great Lakes to meet the unprecedented demand for steel created by the first truly global war. As a whole, 266.7 million gross tons of iron ore was carried on the lakes during the 4-year conflict, an achievement representing nearly 28.3 million gross tons more than that transported during the previous 6 seasons combined. In fact, the amount of ore carried during World War I exceeded the entire ore float for the first 8 years of the twentieth century. Despite experiencing a significant decline in demand during the 1921 shipping season that resulted in the movement of only 22.3 million gross tons of iron ore, the trade remained relatively strong throughout the balance of the 1920s.

On January 17, 1925, the American Ship Building Company launched the steamer *Philip D. Block* at Lorain, Ohio. While built for Hutchinson & Company's Pioneer Steamship Company, this ship took the name of one of the principal founders of Inland Steel and was largely committed to serving that company's bulk transportation needs. Entering service on April 11, 1925, this 600-foot steamer spent much of its time delivering cargoes into Indiana Harbor with trips into other destinations taking place as the need arose.

While the circumstances behind this particular arrangement remain unknown, the possibility exists that Inland Steel's inexperience with new ship construction prompted it to enlist the assistance of Hutchinson & Company during the middle of 1924 to build and operate the *Philip D. Block*. If this was in fact the case, then it represents an extension to the close working relationship developed between the two organizations, which included the actual formation of the Inland Steamship Company some thirteen years earlier.

On the morning of February 1, 1927, a crowd gathered at the American Ship Building Company's yard at Lorain, Ohio to witness the midday launch of Inland Steel's first new ship. Named to honor the steelmaker's chairman of the board, this steamer measured 621 feet in length, 64 feet in beam, and 33 feet in depth. As such, the *L. E. Block* was one of the largest ships on the lakes when it embarked upon it maiden voyage on April 14, 1927 by departing Toledo, Ohio with a load of coal for delivery to Indiana Harbor.

Although constructed to carry raw materials into Indiana Harbor, the Hutchinson management agreement saw this steamer occasionally employed on trade routes outside those required by Inland Steel. One such occasion took place just within a week of the *L. E. Block* entering service when a strong demand for coal during the spring of 1927 resulted in this vessel loading one such cargo at Sandusky, Ohio over the weekend of April 23-24 for delivery to Buffalo, New York.

Later that same year, the American Ship Building Company delivered the *Harry Coulby* (2) to the Interlake Steamship Company. Sharing similar design characteristics to the *L. E. Block*, this ship measured 10 feet

In addition to being the first ship constructed for Inland Steel, the *L. E. Block* was one of the largest ships on the Great Lakes when it entered service in 1927. (Author's Collection)

longer in length and 1 foot wider in beam. With nearly identical carrying capacities, the *L. E. Block* and *Harry Coulby* (2) soon entered into a race to establish a series of Great Lakes iron ore cargo records that lasted well into the 1940s. During World War II, these ships faced new competition in this endeavor from Canada Steamship's *Lemoyne* (1) when that steamer left its familiar coal and grain trade patterns to engage in the movement of iron ore into American ports to assist the war effort.

Launched in 1926, the *Lemoyne* (1) was the first vessel built for service on the Great Lakes with a 70-foot beam, which combined with a 633-foot length and 29-foot 3-inch depth made it a strong contender in the movement of bulk cargoes on the upper lakes. Although eclipsed in both size and capacity in 1942 by the five units of Pittsburgh Steamship's Super class, these three vessels remained among the largest on the Great Lakes until the *Wilfred Sykes* entered service in 1950.

In 1928, Inland Steel's progression towards a vertical integration of its steel making operation resulted in the purchase of the White Marble Lime Company and plans to open a stone quarry near Manistique in Michigan's Upper Peninsula. The following year, the steelmaker's newly formed Inland Lime and Stone Company built a harbor on Lake Michigan fifty-five miles west of the Straits of Mackinac that it named Port Inland. Following the construction of a crushing plant at the quarry near Huntspur in 1930, the first shipment of limestone from the new ship loading facility took place on November 14 of that year aboard steamer *Joseph Block*.

The years of the Great Depression were to have a lasting effect upon the Great Lakes shipping industry. As the single most important commodity in the production of steel, the movement of iron ore between Great Lakes ports on an annual basis serves as an indicator to the general health of the domestic steel industry. Although lake carriers moved 65,204,600 gross tons of iron ore on the lakes during the 1929 season, an amount higher than any previous year, the global economy stood on the brink of the most severe and prolonged financial depression it had ever experienced. By the following year, iron ore shipments had declined by nearly 29-percent as the market for steel products collapsed. While 1931 proved an even more dismal year for commerce on the Great Lakes with shipments of iron ore amounting to only 23.5 million gross tons, it proved pale in comparison to the devastating 1932 season in which the ore trade had fallen to a paltry 3.6 million gross tons. It is interesting to note that the entire ore float recorded for that season, the lowest ever experienced since the 1880s, is just slightly in excess to the amount of cargo carried by a single thousand-footer today during a regular operating season. Despite iron ore shipments rebounding to 21.6 million gross tons in 1933, it was not until 1936 that shipments of this key steel making ingredient was to exceed 40 million gross tons.

Despite the hardships faced by the steel industry, the Inland Steel Company made a series of investments to expand its steel making capabilities during this timeframe. This included some $30 million spent on expansion between 1929 and 1932, the largest component of which was the construction of a new hot strip mill at a cost of $15 million. Although failing to make a profit in 1932, Inland Steel nonetheless operated at a quarter of its capacity—a feat unmatched in the industry during that particular year.

The astonishing decline in demand for the movement of raw materials on the Great Lakes caused by the Depression led to many shipping companies idling a large number of ships due to lack of work. Unsurprisingly, these same conditions brought about an abrupt halt of all vessel construction with no new ships added to the U.S. lakes fleet between 1931 and 1937.

With employment scarce on shore, masters often accepted positions aboard the few operational vessels as mates while former mates sailed as deckhands. Not immune to this downward progression below decks, many engineers found themselves relegated to the duties of coal passers. Although economic conditions began to improve significantly during 1935, the Depression had left an indelible mark upon the Great Lakes shipping industry. In fact, had it not been for a depressed scrap market, it is likely that several ships would not have survived this period.

As part of its strategy to expand its market share, the Inland Steel Company merged with Joseph T. Ryerson & Son, Inc. of Chicago, Illinois in 1935. This transaction resulted in the steelmaker gaining control of the largest steel distributor in the United States, thereby placing it into a better position to compete with the United States Steel Corporation. This merger also resulted in the president of the warehousing chain, Edward L. Ryerson, becoming vice chairman of the board of Inland Steel before rising to the post of chairman of the board five years later in 1940.

At the end of the 1935 shipping season, the Inland Steamship Company consisted of the steamers *Joseph Block*, *L. E. Block*, and the *N. F. Leopold*. Remaining relatively unchanged since its founding, Inland Steel's fleet had increased in size by only one steamer during its first twenty-four years of existence. Within a few short months, however, this fleet was to undergo a significant reorganization as it entered a period of expansion symbolized by further acquisitions, significant rebuilding programs, and new vessel construction.

Chapter Two
Reorganization and Expansion 1936-1960

During a special meeting held on April 3, 1936, the stockholders of the Inland Steamship Company approved a resolution to discontinue further business and to dispose of the corporation's property and assets following the payment of outstanding debts. Thirteen days later, the company announced plans to place its three steamers up for sale at an auction scheduled for May 1, 1936 at Chicago, Illinois. Despite the outward appearance of these events, the Inland Steel Company had no intention to liquidate its marine fleet interests. Rather, the purpose of the public sale was to bring the three ships into direct ownership of the steelmaker. As such, the Inland Steel Company simply outbid all of the others parties in attendance at the auction to purchase the *Joseph Block*, *L. E. Block*, and *N. F. Leopold* with a winning bid of $1,075,330.

Having retained its 32 ½ percent stake in the Inland Steamship Company, Hutchinson & Company received proceeds from the corporation's liquidation in direct proportion to its ownership. Despite this major restructuring, the operation of the vessels remained essentially unchanged with Inland Steel entering into a new agreement with Hutchinson to manage its fleet.

It was within this same timeframe that Inland Steel also purchased the *Philip D. Block* from Hutchinson's Pioneer Steamship Company. As noted earlier, this vessel had been primarily committed to supplying Inland's needs since its 1925 commissioning, and therefore its acquisition was a natural progression in the steelmaker's effort to expand its fleet. Second in size only to the *L. E. Block*, the addition of the *Philip D. Block* increased the combined single trip carrying capacity of the fleet to 48,900 gross tons.

The *Philip D. Block* following its purchase by the Inland Steel Company. (Author's Collection)

From an appearance standpoint, one of the most noticeable changes following the reorganization was the replacement of the Inland Steamship Company lettering on the bows of the *Joseph Block*, *L. E. Block*, and *N. F. Leopold* with the words Inland Steel Company. In addition, the *Philip D. Block* lost its Pioneer Steamship Company color scheme when workers repainted the steamer to reflect its new ownership.

Although 1936 proved a banner year with combined total of 114,414,748 net tons worth of iron ore, coal, stone, and grain being moved by lake freighters across the Great Lakes, the highest such level since 1930, heavy ice caused considerable delays at the beginning of the shipping season. With loading ports on Lake Superior remaining in winter's grip, officials delayed the opening of the locks at Sault Ste. Marie, Michigan for nearly two weeks as they awaited the spring thaw. It was not until April 29 that the steamer *Pontiac* (2) of the Cleveland-Cliffs Steamship Company opened the 1936 navigational season at the Soo Locks when it passed upbound into Lake Superior followed closely behind by fleet mates *J. H. Sheadle* (2), and *Ishpeming* (2). During a season that witnessed 44.8 million gross tons of ore shipped on the lakes, the four vessels of Inland Steel fleet continued operating in their long established pattern of moving raw materials into Indiana Harbor.

As Europe marched inevitably towards war during the late 1930s, the movement of iron ore on the lakes began a period of growth in response to the domestic steel industry increasing production to meet the demand generated by the specter of another global conflict. By 1940, shipments of ore had topped 63.7 million gross tons, the third highest level ever reached up to that time. Near the end of the season, however, the Great Lakes suffered one of its most severe fall storms since the 1913 Storm. Dubbed the Armistice Day Storm as it unleashed its fury on November 11, 1940, the anniversary of the end of the First World War, this weather system produced high winds and heavy snow as it passed through the Midwest.

Downbound on Lake Michigan with a load of stone destined for Indiana Harbor, the *Joseph Block* was one of a number of ships caught in the storm. Under the command of Captain Howard Kizer, the *Block* was sailing down the eastern shore of the lake when the wind suddenly shifted from east to southwest. Battling increasing winds that eventually reached 70-mph, Kizer turned his ship towards Milwaukee to reach the opposite shore of the turbulent lake. With two windows smashed in by heavy seas, the men in the pilothouse struggled to maintain control of their ship as ice began coating the ship's navigational equipment. Following a 15-hour battle on Lake Michigan, the *Joseph Block* arrived at

Indiana Harbor on the evening of November 12, 1936 with its crew lucky to have survived the ordeal with just a few minor bruises. In the days immediately following the Armistice Day Storm, a press photograph of Captain Kizer posing in front of the *Block's* ice encrusted pilothouse ran in newspapers across the country.

While the crew of the *Joseph Block* managed to reach port, some those aboard other vessels struggling on Lake Michigan in the sudden storm were far less fortunate. Having passed through the Straits of Mackinac during the afternoon of November 11, 1940, Interlake Steamship's *William B. Davock,* and the Canadian flagged *Anna C. Minch* of the Western Navigation Company both foundered with all hands off the Michigan coast. In addition to the 56 killed in those two wrecks, the storm also sank the fish tugs *Indian* and *Richard H.* with the loss of 8 additional lives. Pushed towards shore by the massive waves, Paterson's *Novadoc* (2) ran aground on a reef just south of Pentwater, Michigan. A few hours later, two men perished when huge waves washed them from the broken deck of the canal-sized freighter while trying to make their way from the stern to the bow.

Entering the Second World War in December of 1941, the United States committed its entire industrial might to the war effort. The insatiable appetite of the nation's blast furnaces generated an unprecedented demand for raw materials. This translated into the Great Lakes shipping fleet carrying tonnages far in excess of anything it had before. The demand for iron ore movement peaked in 1942 when lake freighters carried an almost unbelievable 92,076,781 gross tons of ore in support of the steel industry. Hauling just over 522 million gross tons of this vital raw material during the war, ships operating on the Great Lakes played a significant role in securing the Allied victory.

During the war, Inland Steel embarked upon a series of programs to expand its steel making capabilities, among which included new blast furnaces and coke ovens. While focusing much of this effort on its manufacturing facilities, the company also invested in its shipping fleet. As part of this process, the fleet's oldest vessel, the *Joseph Block*, received new boilers in 1941. Just four years later, this steamer underwent a more extensive reconstruction involving the installation of new tank tops and side tanks along with the replacement of its original telescoping hatch covers with single piece hatches. During its third major improvement project completed during the 1940s, the *Joseph Block* had its boilers converted from coal to oil-fired in 1947.

In 1943, the *N. F. Leopold* was renamed *E. J. Block* to honor Emanuel J. Block, a son of Inland Steel founder Joseph Block who had died in March of 1939 after serving as a company vice president. In 1946, this 38-year old ship went to the American Ship Building Company's Lorain yard for conversion into a diesel-electric motor vessel. Completed at a cost of $1.25 million, this ambitious reconstruction project also included new fore and aft cabins and improved auxiliary equipment. Emerging from the shipyard in its new configuration on September 18, 1946 to conduct sea trials on Lake Erie, the *E. J. Block* reentered service the following day when it sailed to load coal at Sandusky, Ohio for Indiana Harbor.

In April of 1946, Inland Steel engaged Hutchinson & Company to act on its behalf to purchase the motor vessel *Steel Chemist* from the American Steel and Wire Company. Built in 1926, this canal-sized vessel was equipped with two deck-mounted cranes capable of loading and offloading finished steel products. With the acquisition of this vessel occurring during a time when rail carriers were lobbying to increase their freight rates from prewar levels, it appears that the management of the Inland Steel Company purchased the *Steel Chemist* to increase its bargaining position in the upcoming negotiations. Shortly after coming under the steelmaker's ownership, the twenty-year old crane vessel was renamed *The Inland*.

On May 8, 1946, *The Inland* sailed on its maiden voyage as a member of the Inland Steel fleet when it departed Indiana Harbor with a cargo of automotive sheet metal bound for delivery to Detroit, Michigan. Commanding the vessel on this initial trip was recently promoted Captain W. S. Walsh of Hammond, Indiana, who had previously served as first mate with the fleet since 1939. Measuring 258′ 3″ in length, *The Inland* had a carrying capacity of 2,900 gross tons and a crew of 25.

Operating independently of the role performed by its fleet mates in providing raw material deliveries to Indiana Harbor, *The Inland* remained part of Inland Steel fleet until its sale in May of 1948 to Transit Tankers & Terminals Ltd. of Montreal, Quebec for conversion into a tanker. Destined to serve nearly another 30 years on the waters of the Great Lakes, this ship retained part of its Inland Steel heritage in the liquid bulk trade by operating first under the name *Transinland* and later *Inland Transport* until its sale for dismantling in 1976.

In a press release dated June 16, 1948, American Ship Building Company President W. H. Gerhauser announced his company entering into a contract with the Inland Steel Company to build the first postwar U.S. flagged ship for service on the Great Lakes. As with other endeavors up to this point in the history of Inland Steel's marine operations, the close working relationship between that firm and Hutchinson & Company played a large role in guiding the project. Designed as the largest and fastest lake freighter ever built up to that time, this ship was to incorporate a number of design innovations that were to influence shipbuilding practices on the lakes throughout the following decade. In addition, it was also the first lake freighter designed with a carrying capacity in excess of 20,000 gross tons of iron ore. Generating considerable fanfare in marine journals and regional newspapers, details of the new ship slowly emerged over the following months. Nearly two months after announcing plans for the steamer's construction, on August 6, 1948, Edward L. Ryerson, chairman of the Inland Steel Company, issued a press statement revealing the new ship was to be named in honor of the steelmaker's current president, Wilfred Sykes.

Born in Palmerston, New Zealand on December 3, 1883, Wilfred Sykes and his family relocated to Australia in 1889. Graduating from the University of Melbourne in 1902, he secured employment with the Australian division of the German electrical company Allgemeine Elektricitats Gesellschaft (AEG). Before leaving this organization in 1908, Wilfred Sykes spent two years working at the company's headquarters in Berlin, Germany. Arriving in the United States the following year, he joined the Westinghouse Corporation before taking a position at the Steel & Tube Company of America as executive engineer in 1920. Joining Inland Steel in 1923, Wilfred Sykes moved steadily up the ranks to become general superintendent of the Indiana Harbor plant in 1927 and finally company president in 1941, a position he held until retiring in 1949.

During the design phase of the project, Inland Steel and American Ship Building enlisted the assistance of Professor Louis A. Baier and Assistant Professor Charles W. Spooner, Jr. of the University of Michigan's Naval Architecture and Marine Engineering Department. While Louis Baier formulated information concerning the vessel's dimensions and power plant characteristics, Charles Spooner worked on the hull design. Utilizing the institution's water test tank at Ann Arbor, Michigan, the research performed by the two professors provided important data that influenced the final design of the *Wilfred Sykes*.

The resulting hull design incorporated a raked stem and a cruiser stern that contrasted sharply to the elliptical stern of traditional lake freighters. First used on the Great Lakes during World War II with the construction of six of the sixteen Maritime class steamers, this stern design reduced water resistance and improved flow characteristics to the propeller.

Although American Ship Building had originally planned to begin construction in August at its Lorain, Ohio yard, workers did not lay the keel for the 678-foot steamer until November 1, 1948. Work progressed smoothly with the *Wilfred Sykes* slowly taking shape along the banks of the Black River throughout the remaining weeks of 1948 and into the following summer. Painted in the new eye-catching color scheme of the Inland Steel fleet, the large steamer slid down the launching ways and into the adjacent flooded dry dock on the morning of June 28, 1949. Casting a pall over the festive nature of that day's ceremonies, however, was the death of a 78-year old spectator that suffered a heart attack just minutes before the launching.

While the *Wilfred Sykes* was under construction, Inland Steel assigned one of its veteran captains, Howard H. Kizer, to serve as its representative at the shipyard as a precursor to his posting as the vessel's first master. As related earlier, Kizer had briefly gained some notoriety in 1940 after guiding the *Joseph Block* through the Armistice Day Storm on Lake Michigan to reach Indiana Harbor. Coming to know nearly every inch of Inland's new steamer during its construction and subsequent sea trials, fate dealt Captain Kizer a cruel hand when he fell seriously ill at Englewood, Florida in March of 1950. Kizer's sudden illness forced Inland Steel to assign another of its veteran captains, George W. Fisher, to command the *Wilfred Sykes* when it began its inaugural season a few weeks later. His health continuing to deteriorate throughout the following months, Howard H.

Kizer died on November 4, 1950 at age 56.

On April 19, 1950, the *Wilfred Sykes* began its maiden voyage when it departed Lorain to load a cargo of coal at Toledo, Ohio for delivery to Indiana Harbor. Widely hailed as "Queen of the Lakes," Inland's new steamer proceeded up the lakes amid great fanfare. While making its passage between Lake Erie and Lake Huron, thousands lined the shoreline of the Detroit and St. Clair rivers to catch a glimpse of the newest behemoth on the lakes. One week after departing the shipyard, the *Wilfred*

An aerial view of the newly constructed *Wilfred Sykes* off Lorain, Ohio. (Author's Collection)

Sykes sailed into Indiana Harbor to offload the first cargo of what has become a long and successful operational career.

Although the *Wilfred Sykes* was the first U.S. flagged carrier built since 1943, it was not the first ship to enter service on the Great Lakes following the end of the Second World War as a handful of canal-sized vessels had joined the Canadian fleet in the years immediately after the war. Launched on August 4, 1949, and beginning its maiden voyage on October 27 of that same year, the 639-foot 6-inch long *Hochelaga* of the Canada Steamship Lines became the first large postwar bulk carrier on the lakes.

With a carrying capacity twice that of Inland Steel's oldest and smallest units, the commissioning of the *Wilfred Sykes* had a profound impact upon the fleet's seasonal tonnage capacity. Increasing the steelmaker's fleet to five bulk carriers, the 21,500 gross ton payload capacity of the new vessel boosted the fleet's single trip capacity to 68,000 gross tons, of which the *Sykes* represented nearly 32% of the total fleet capacity. In addition, the faster speed characteristics of the new turbine powered steamer permitted it to complete several more trips between loading ports on Lake Superior and Indiana Harbor each shipping season in comparison to its slower fleet mates.

Unsurprisingly, the *Wilfred Sykes* quickly proved itself a

prodigious iron ore carrier upon entering service. Its first season proved so successful that by mid-October the revolutionary steamer had completed 33 round trips between Indiana Harbor and loading ports on Lake Superior, a number equivalent to that of a normal season for other vessels in the Inland Steel fleet. Despite there still being two months remaining in the shipping season, the *Wilfred Sykes* had already carried 655,930 gross tons of iron ore, including a record 20,779 gross ton cargo delivered to the steelmaker's plant on October 3, 1950. All but one of these ore cargoes were loaded at Superior,

The *Wilfred Sykes* became a popular subject for postcards following its entry into service in April of 1950. This particular example remains one of the most common postcards connected with Great Lakes shipping to this day. (Author's Collection)

Wisconsin, the sole exception being a single load taken on at Marquette, Michigan during this vessel's first voyage into Lake Superior.

By the immediate postwar period, the color scheme of the Inland Steel fleet had evolved to consist of dark red hulls, white cabins, and black stacks. A little more than halfway up the height of the stack was a red band with a white diamond logo that had a letter "I" located at its center. On each side of the hull were the words "INLAND STEEL" separated by a large Inland Steel diamond logo. The new color scheme applied to the *Wilfred Sykes* was one of the most elaborate ever given to a lake freighter. Painted reddish-brown, the new hull colors retained the Inland Steel billboard lettering while also incorporating a wide white stripe that ran completely around the ship just a few feet below the level of the spar deck. The forecastle and stern of the *Sykes* received distinctive white and gray bands, with the vessel's name and homeport painted in black lettering. The application of gray bands extended to the white cabins, thereby giving Inland Steel's new steamer an even more striking appearance. Painted white at its base, the revised stack markings featured a wide stainless steel band with a red Inland Steel diamond logo. With the top of the stack painted red, a thin dark blue stripe located immediately below the silver band rounded out the new markings.

Despite the laborious nature of maintaining such a paint scheme, a task made difficult by regular visits to the acrid industrial environment at Indiana Harbor and dusty loading docks, the new colors were soon adopted fleet wide. The vibrant appearance of Inland Steel vessels instantly made them one of the most recognizable and popular fleets on the Great Lakes. While altered nearly fifty years later by a change in the steel company's ownership, the color scheme pioneered by the *Wilfred Sykes* has remained relatively intact to this day.

In the years immediately following World War II, the demand for raw material movement on the Great Lakes remained strong as the nation entered into a period of substantial economic and industrial growth. While the Korean War greatly attributed to the heavy seasonal tonnages experienced at the beginning of the 1950s, a robust demand for automobiles and consumer goods also contributed in shaping the domestic steel industry during the early years of that decade.

With relatively few ships built since the Depression, several shipping companies operating on the Great Lakes faced the dilemma of possessing fleets with units becoming increasingly obsolete at a time of healthy demand. These circumstances led to a decade long period of shipbuilding that resulted in thirty-four new freight vessels joining the U.S. flagged fleet between 1950

The Wilfred Sykes Passing Port Huron, Michigan and Sarnia, Ontario

PHOTO BY RUSSELL E. SAWYER   1C-H1727

Another linen postcard view of the *Wilfred Sykes*, this time portraying the vessel making its maiden voyage up the St. Clair River at Port Huron, Michigan. Produced by the Port Huron News Co., this card shows the steamer just as it was about to pass beneath the Blue Water Bridge. (Author's Collection)

and 1960. With the region's shipyards flooded to capacity with orders at the beginning of the 1950s, some shipping companies looked outside the lakes for additional tonnage. Such endeavors resulted in the construction of three lake steamers on the East Coast and the conversion of seven saltwater vessels for use on the Great Lakes between 1950 and 1953.

Although Inland Steel slowed the expansion of its steel making capacity during the early 1950s, the company

31

remained committed to maintaining an efficient fleet to supply its raw material transportation needs. In addition to commissioning the *Wilfred Sykes*, the steelmaker continued its program of fleet modernization with a series of mid-life upgrades that permitted its older vessels remain viable carriers. The cargo statistics for 1951 reflect the increased demand for steel production during this period. During that particular shipping season, the ships of the Inland Steel fleet, along with those of other shipping firms, delivered a record 5,139,761 gross tons of iron ore and 1,462,344 net tons of limestone to the steelmaker's mill at Indiana Harbor.

In December of 1950, Carl B. Jacobs, Inland Steel's fleet and raw materials manager, announced his company's plan to rebuild the *Philip D. Block* to a length of 672 feet with the addition of a new 72-foot mid-section. This reconstruction, which took place at the American Ship Building Company's South Chicago yard during the 1950-51 winter layup, raised the *Block*'s carrying capacity from 12,000 to 15,000 gross tons, an increase of 25%. In its newly lengthened state, the twenty-six year old steamer departed Indiana Harbor for Superior, Wisconsin on April 30, 1951.

The increased length of the *Philip D. Block* brought it to within just six feet of the *Wilfred Sykes*, thus making it the second longest ship on the Great Lakes at the time. This steamer held that title until September of the following year when the 678-foot *John O. McKellar* (2) of the Colonial Steamships, Ltd. fleet equaled the length of the *Sykes* before the 714-foot *Joseph H. Thompson* surpassed both of these vessels two months later to become the longest ship on the Great Lakes. Although destined to remain one of the longest ships on the Great Lakes for several years, the *Philip D. Block*'s carrying capacity was still 900 gross tons less than its shorter, but wider and deeper, fleet mate *L. E. Block*.

In the fall of 1952, the *Philip D. Block* entered the second phase of its modernization program by returning to the American Ship Building Company's South Chicago yard for a repowering. This process involved the replacement of the vessel's original triple-expansion engine with a new 4,950 shaft horsepower Westinghouse Electric steam turbine. At the same time, workers also installed oil-fired boilers along with new pumps, generators, and auxiliary equipment. In addition to the reconstruction of the after cabins with improved crew accommodations, work at the shipyard also included repainting the *Philip D. Block* in the unique Inland Steel color scheme first applied to the *Wilfred Sykes*.

On July 11, 1953, the *Philip D. Block* conducted a 10 ½-hour run on Lake Michigan to test out its new power plant. Not encountering any major difficulties during the sea trials, this steamer reentered service in the ore trade the following week. Estimates published at the time indicate that the 20% increase in speed provided by the new engines cut an average of 15 hours off each of the vessel's round trips between Indiana Harbor and Superior, Wisconsin. Officials at Inland Steel projected that such an increase in performance would permit the *Philip D. Block* to complete five additional trips per season.

That same year saw the completion of the fleet's last major reconstruction project during this period when the *L. E. Block* received a steam turbine identical to that installed in the *Philip D. Block* and two oil-fired Babcock & Wilcox boilers. With the repowering of these two steamers, the Inland Steel fleet became one of the few firms on the lakes at the time to adopt the exclusive use of oil rather than coal to fuel its vessels.

Even as war raged on the Korean Peninsula, a labor dispute concerning wage increases simmered in America's steel industry. When the United Steelworkers of America (USWA) threatened a strike by its members in December of 1951 after industry leaders refused to reach an agreement, President Harry S. Truman ordered the matter taken to the War Stabilization Board. Following nearly four months of fruitless discussion and with the threat of a strike looming heavily on the horizon, Truman took the unprecedented step of nationalizing the country's steel mills in April 1952. Within hours of the U.S. Supreme Court ruling this seizure as being unconstitutional on June 2, the nation's steel industry came to a standstill when 600,000 steel workers walked off their jobs to begin a work stoppage lasting 53 days.

The heavy depletion of raw material stockpiles over the following winter and favorable ice conditions allowed the 1953 shipping season to begin somewhat earlier than usual with the first iron ore loadings commencing in late March. Early season activity included the *E. J. Block* opening the port of Escanaba, Michigan on March 30, followed by the *Joseph Block* becoming the first ship of the season at Marquette, Michigan on April 3. Buoyed by high demand, the iron ore trade remained strong throughout the season with a monthly loading record of 15,000,000 gross tons achieved for the first time in August of that year. As the shipping season neared its end, the *L. E. Block* closed the Canadian National ore dock at Port Arthur, Ontario on November 16, while the *Wilfred Sykes* loaded the last ore cargo at Superior, Wisconsin four days later. Despite the absence of any loadings during the month of December, lake freighters carried 95,844,449 gross tons of iron ore during the 1953 season, the highest ever achieved in the history of commerce on the Great Lakes.

On July 1, 1956, the ongoing conflict between the steel industry and organized labor continued with the beginning of another nationwide strike. This work stoppage prompted the idling of all five Inland Steel vessels, one of which went into dry dock for work, until the end of the month when the steel companies and the USWA reached an agreement to end the walkout.

That same month, the fleet entered into a new chapter of its history when Inland Steel informed Hutchinson & Company of its intention to end the long-standing fleet management agreement between the two firms at the conclusion of the 1956 shipping season. Having begun concurrent with Inland Steel's first vessel acquisitions in 1911, this arrangement had lasted 45 years. Despite this decision, the steelmaker continued to allocate Hutchinson's Pioneer Steamship Company a portion of its seasonal raw material transportation requirements.

During the summer of 1959, another nationwide strike by the USWA once again shut down steel mills across the country. Lasting nearly four months, the labor dispute led to the idling of several ships operating on the Great Lakes and was to prove particularly devastating to the domestic steel industry by opening the U.S. market to cheaper imported steel. Playing a significant role in the continuing decline of steel production in the United States, this strike harmed both the steel companies and their employees alike.

On February 25, 1953, the Inland Steel Company announced a $50 million mining project involving high-grade iron ore deposits located under Steep Rock Lake near Atikokan, Ontario approximately 120 miles west of Port Arthur, Ontario. As part of this endeavor, the steelmaker established a Canadian subsidiary, the Caland Ore Company, Ltd., to lease one of the several ore bodies owned by Steep Rock Iron Mines, Ltd. for a period of 99 years. Acknowledging that the work necessary to drain Steep Rock Lake before the mining of ore could begin was to take at least 7 years to complete, Philip D. Block, Jr., Inland's vice president in charge of raw materials, described the project to reporters as, "...the biggest Inland has ever entered into."

Work continued steadily throughout the balance of the decade, with the departure of the first trainload from the mine coinciding with the Caland project's formal dedication on May 3, 1960. Under the command of Captain Wilfred J. Lemcke, the steamer *John O. McKellar* (2) arrived at Indiana Harbor with the first load of Caland ore at 10 o'clock in the morning of May 11, 1960. Following a brief ceremony aboard the vessel to commemorate the occasion, clamshell buckets began discharging the 18,500 gross ton ore cargo loaded two days earlier at Port Arthur. Inland Steel vessels were to remain regular visitors to Port Arthur, and later Thunder Bay, for nearly another 20 years.

On December 18, 1958, Inland Steel announced the awarding of a contract to Manitowoc Shipbuilding, Incorporated of Manitowoc, Wisconsin to build a 730-foot bulk freighter at a cost of $8 million. At the same time, Philip D. Block, Jr. revealed the steamer's name as *Edward L. Ryerson* in honor of the company's former chairman from 1940 until his retirement in 1953. That same month, Inland Steel released a press photograph of a model depicting its new vessel. This image revealed a far more aggressive approach to the use of streamlined features than that used on the *Wilfred Sykes*.

Destined to be the last lake vessel ever built at Manitowoc, workers laid the keel of the *Ryerson* during a ceremony on April 20, 1959 attended by the steamer's namesake along with a delegation from Inland Steel and representatives from the shipyard. Also in attendance at the keel laying celebrations that day were Carl Tripp, a naval architect from the ship's design firm, H. C. Downer & Associates, and Karl Brocken a well-known industrial designer responsible for the bulk carrier's unique styling.

At 11:58 am on January 21, 1960, the *Edward L. Ryerson* slid down the ways and into the cold waters of the Manitowoc River. Although by far the largest ship ever built at that city, several veteran observers noted that

Inland's new vessel did not create as large of wave as those of previous launches at the shipyard. Regardless, the water surge created by the *Ryerson* threw several large chunks of ice into the Manitowoc municipal dock across the river that caused considerable damage to the structure.

Built specifically to carry iron ore, the design of the *Edward L. Ryerson* incorporated four cargo holds with a collective capacity of 27,000 gross tons. The holds incorporated flat sides to speed unloading times while also reducing the danger of damage by the clamshell buckets of shore based equipment. Despite incorporating a styling with many features perhaps more akin those found on a cruise ship, the design characteristics of the *Edward L. Ryerson* made it one of the most efficient ore carriers of its day.

Throughout the spring and into the summer of 1960, workers continued the construction of the *Ryerson* with the installation of its cabins, deck equipment, and distinctive stainless steel smoke stack. Painted in Inland Steel colors, the steamer was nearly finished by the middle of June as it sat in the shipyard awaiting a move upriver to a lakefront dock in anticipation of its upcoming sea trials. This move took place on July 28 with four tugs maneuvering the *Ryerson* through the confines of Manitowoc River and its narrow bridge openings over an

The unique profile of the *Edward L. Ryerson* is apparent in this view of the vessel loading ore at the Great Northern Railway dock at Superior, Wisconsin during the early 1960s. (Author's Collection)

operation lasting 4 ½ hours in length. Four days later, on August 1, 1960, the *Edward L. Ryerson* successfully completed its sea trials in Lake Michigan, thus paving the way for its entry into operational service.

On August 4, 1960, the *Edward L. Ryerson* cleared Manitowoc on its maiden voyage to load iron ore at Escanaba, Michigan for delivery to Indiana Harbor. After unloading its initial cargo, the new flagship of the Inland Steel fleet settled into a regular trading pattern of transporting ore from loading facilities on Lake Superior to its owner's homeport. While the *Edward L. Ryerson* was under construction, Inland Steel officials spoke of employing their new ship in carrying ore through the St. Lawrence Seaway from the steelmaker's mining interests in Canada's Labrador region. Despite initial reports that such service would begin during the mid-1960s, it was not until 2007, or nearly 50 years later, that this ship first transited that waterway system.

With the commissioning of the *Edward L. Ryerson*, the single trip capacity of the Inland Steel fleet exceeded 100,000 gross tons for the first time in its history. Perhaps even more remarkable is the increased efficiency offered by postwar lake vessel designs as the combined payload capabilities of the *Wilfred Sykes* and *Edward L. Ryerson* represented nearly half of the fleet's capacity at the beginning of the 1960s.

Investing in the construction of two new ships and the extensive modernization of four others as it strove to meet postwar demands, the years between 1945 and 1960 proved the most dynamic period in the history of the Inland Steel fleet.

Chapter Three
Changing Times 1961-1979

The opening of the St. Lawrence Seaway in 1959 proved devastating to several independent U.S. flagged fleets operating on the Great Lakes. With Canadian shipping firms taking full advantage of hauling grain down the Seaway and returning with backhauls of iron ore, the domestic trade routes relied upon by these smaller fleets faced direct outside competition for the first time. One firm to suffer heavily from this shift in traffic patterns was the Pioneer Steamship Company, which by the early months of 1962 had set plans to cease operations in motion.

While Pioneer supplied some of Inland Steel's seasonal floating requirements, the drastic decline in the grain trade formerly routed through Buffalo, New York, but now largely bypassing that city, hit this fleet especially hard. In addition, the steelmaker was to begin receiving iron ore from Labrador following its 1959 investment in the Wabush Iron Co. Ltd., of which it held a 10% stake. With Canadian vessels delivering this ore on their return visits to the lakes, Inland Steel had no need to employ its own vessels or charter outside U.S. flagged tonnage to carry these cargoes.

On May 17, 1962, the Pioneer Steamship Company announced its liquidation plans with the sale of the *Clarence B. Randall* (1) and *Pioneer Challenger* to the Oglebay Norton Company for $6.2 million. This report, however, came as little surprise to the shipping community as Pioneer had previously made progress in that direction by selling its largest vessel, *Charles L. Hutchinson* (3), to the Ford Motor Company in March of that year.

The dissolution of this long-standing shipping fleet provided the Inland Steel Company with an opportunity to acquire the 552-foot long *J. J. Sullivan* in May of 1962 for $325,000. Launched in 1907, this steamer had spent its entire career as a member of the Hutchinson's family marine interests by first sailing for the Superior Steamship Company before its 1915 transfer to the Pioneer Steamship Company. Prior to its purchase by Inland Steel, the *Sullivan* had been steadily engaged in the movement of raw materials into the steelmaker's Indiana Harbor plant for several years. In addition, this ship also became the last coal-fired vessel ever operated by the Inland Steel fleet.

Repowered in 1950 with a 2,400 indicated horsepower Skinner Unaflow engine, the acquisition of the *J. J. Sullivan* increased the Inland Steel fleet to seven vessels.

The *J. J. Sullivan* underway in transitional colors following its purchase by the Inland Steel Company during the 1962 season. (Author's Collection)

This was, in fact, the largest number of ships ever operated at one time by the steelmaker up to this time. While only boosting the fleet's single trip capacity by an additional 10,200 gross tons, this steamer's relatively small size in an era of increasingly larger ships proved one of its most beneficial assets. Sharing a beam width identical to those of the *E. J. Block* and *Joseph Block*, this vessel was able to deliver cargoes to Inland's Dock #3, which was inaccessible to larger carriers in the fleet due to a number of narrow railroad bridge openings over the

Indiana Harbor Ship Canal.

The layout of Inland Steel's docking facilities at Indiana Harbor necessitated the establishment of a transshipment operation to move raw materials brought into the industrial complex by vessels too large to navigate past the bridges. These ships unloaded at Dock #2, which is located just inside the harbor at the entrance of the Indiana Harbor Ship Canal. To overcome this problem, Inland Steel employed its smaller vessels to shuttle raw materials between that dock and Dock #3's location upstream of the bridges. The vessels assigned to this transshipment operation delivered about 10,000 gross tons to Dock #3 on each round trip.

Entering operation immediately, the *J. J. Sullivan* sailed in transitional colors for a short time while slowly gaining its new owner's unique color scheme. Service under its original name in the fleet did not last long, however, as that same year Inland Steel renamed this steamer *Clarence B. Randall* (2).

Assigned to the shuttle run over short distance between Inland's Dock #2 and Dock #3 for a good part of the shipping season, the *Clarence B. Randall* (2) made occasional trips to Escanaba to and Lake Superior to load ore. In addition to the Inland vessels engaged in transshipment operations at Indiana Harbor during this period, Misener Transportation Limited also employed its

550-foot long *Royalton* (1) in delivering Canadian ore to the size restricted Dock #3.

By the late 1940s, the once seemingly endless deposits of high-grade ore on the Mesabi Range that had supplied the nation's steel mills during an era of great industrial expansion and two world wars was nearing exhaustion. This situation prompted the commercial development of taconite pelletizing operations to process the still abundant low-grade ores present in the Lake Superior region. Although such endeavors stretched back to a failed attempt to market taconite produced by a commercial concentrating plant located near Babbitt, Minnesota during the early 1920s, the expenses associated with this operation resulted in prices unable to compete with low-cost conventionally mined ores. With taconite pellets destined to dominate the future movement of iron ore on the Great Lakes, the development of this industry during the 1950s prompted the construction of two new ports on Lake Superior.

Taconite pellets provided shipping companies two major advantages over irregular shaped natural ore. First, the marble like physical characteristics of taconite made it easily handled by self-unloading vessels capable of discharging their cargoes at any dock and at rates often exceeding that of shore side equipment. Secondly, since the pellets were not prone to freezing as is the case with natural ore, shippers could extend their season later in the year when the onset of winter had previously shutdown the loading docks on the upper lakes between late November and early December. These two factors, along with the steady decline of the domestic steel industry, contributed heavily to the significant downsizing of the Great Lakes shipping industry in the decades to come.

Demonstrating the ability to ship taconite during the onset of winter, the *Wilfred Sykes* loaded the final ore cargo of the 1966 shipping season at Escanaba on December 23 of that year. This shipment surpassed the previous late season benchmark for ore loading established on December 20, 1959. Remarking upon the longevity of the 1966 season, Inland Steel officials

The *L. E. Block* downbound in the St. Marys River.
(M. J. Brown photo)

credited the ability to load taconite in freezing weather and its widespread use in American blast furnaces as the primary reasons behind the record setting shipment.

At 4:30 in the morning of May 22, 1968, the *Joseph Block* ran aground near Plum Island in the Porte des Morts Passage connecting Lake Michigan and Green Bay. En route to Escanaba to load a cargo of taconite at the time, the *Block* immediately began taking on water through its punctured hull. Freed some twelve hours later with the assistance of Roen Steamship's tug *Arrow*, the 61-year old steamer proceeded under its own power to Manitowoc, Wisconsin. A subsequent dry-docking at the Manitowoc Shipbuilding yard revealed extensive bottom damage. Deeming the cost of repairs as being too expensive given the vessel's elderly age, Inland Steel surrendered the *Joseph Block* to its underwriters. This steamer received a lucky reprieve from the scrap yard, however, when the Lake Shipping Company purchased it in June of that year. Repaired at American Ship Building's South Chicago yard, this vessel became a member of the Kinsman Marine Transit Company fleet in June of 1969 as the *George M. Steinbrenner* (2). Serving in the bulk commodity trades, this ship operated until its final layup in 1977 and subsequent sale for scrapping during the summer of the following year.

Beginning with the 1961 shipping season when lake

The motor vessel *E. J. Block* upbound at Mission Point on the
St. Marys River. (M. J. Brown photo)

carriers moved 60.9 million gross tons of iron ore on the
lakes, this trade grew steadily throughout the balance of
the decade, with the exception of a slight decline during
the 1967 season, to peak at 86.3 million gross tons in 1969.
The late 1960s and early 1970s proved an optimistic time
for the domestic steel industry. A strong demand for ore
movements reflected this prosperous period by reaching
a high point of 94,545,275 gross tons in 1973, an amount
exceeded only by the benchmark 1953 season. Prompted
by forecasts predicting the nation's steel industry
required an additional 25 million additional tons of
capacity by the beginning of the following decade, the
management of Inland Steel announced a $2 billion

49

expansion program in September of 1974 with the stated goal of boosting the company's steel manufacturing capacity nearly 20% by 1980. Extending over a ten-year period, this plan called for the Indiana Harbor Works to add 1.6 million tons of capacity by 1984.

Following the commissioning of the *Arthur B. Homer* and *Edward L. Ryerson* in 1960, new American construction on the Great Lakes came to an abrupt halt. In fact, the balance of the decade was to only witness five saltwater conversions join the U.S. fleet. During the late 1960s and early 1970s, however, a number of American shipping companies began looking at modernizing their fleets with new vessels. As the locks at Sault Ste. Marie, Michigan had generally influenced the dimensions of lake freighters since the late 1800s, several of these firms directed much of their effort toward building a new class of carriers that took advantage of the new Poe Lock. Opening in 1969, the dimensions of this lock allowed ships measuring up to 1,000 feet in length and 105 feet in beam to pass between the waters of Lake Superior and Lake Huron.

Whereas, the *Edward L. Ryerson* and *Arthur B. Homer* represented the pinnacle of U.S. flagged traditional Great Lakes bulk carrier design, the new era of ship construction beginning during the early 1970s optimized efficiency above all else. In 1972, the first two super carriers joined the fleet when the 1000-foot long *Stewart J. Cort* and the slightly shorter *Roger Blough* embarked on their maiden voyages. As the first thousand-foot vessel on the Great Lakes, the *Stewart J. Cort* quickly proved itself by loading a record 49,343 gross tons of taconite at Taconite Harbor, Minnesota for Burns Harbor, Indiana on its maiden voyage. The economic advantages offered by this new class of carrier becomes self evident when considering that Inland Steel's newest and largest vessel at the time, the *Edward L. Ryerson*, could only carry a maximum of 27,500 gross tons of ore, or only 47% of the *Cort*'s 58,000 gross ton carrying capacity.

Unlike many of its counterparts operating ships on the Great Lakes, Inland Steel did not lengthen any of its existing vessels during the 1970s. Regardless, it did send the *Wilfred Sykes* to Fraser Shipyards in Superior, Wisconsin at the end of the 1974 shipping season for conversion into a self-unloader. Emerging from the shipyard during the first week of July 1975, this steamer loaded its first cargo as a self-unloading vessel at the nearby Burlington Northern ore docks. In addition to eliminating its reliance on shore based unloading equipment, this conversion also allowed the *Wilfred Sykes* to deliver cargoes to ports outside its owner's direct requirements. This increased flexibility was to pay huge dividends in the years to come.

Even as the conversion of the *Wilfred Sykes* neared completion, workers at the Bay Shipbuilding Corporation in Sturgeon Bay, Wisconsin began construction of what became the last ship ever built for the Inland Steel Company. Launched as that yard's Hull #715 on February 26, 1976, work continued on this 728-foot long diesel powered freighter throughout the following spring and summer. Christened as the *Joseph L. Block* on June 29, 1976, this ship entered service on August 15 of that year when it departed the shipyard bound for Escanaba, Michigan. Loading 32,607 gross tons of pellets at Escanaba for delivery to its owner's steel mill at Indiana Harbor on its maiden voyage, this vessel set a record for

The *Wilfred Sykes* arriving at Indiana Harbor shortly following its conversion into a self-unloader. (Author's Collection)

the largest cargo ever carried by an Inland Steel vessel up to that time.

Like other ships that began emerging from Great Lakes shipyards during the early 1970s, the design of the *Joseph L. Block* incorporated an all cabins aft design emphasizing productivity and maximum carrying capacity. While this utilitarian approach discarded many of the aesthetic features found in previous vessels, it proved highly successful in establishing a new benchmark in the efficient movement of raw materials on the inland seas. A comparison between the *Joseph L. Block* and the similarly sized *Edward L. Ryerson* built just sixteen years earlier at the end of a decade-long period of new U.S. flagged ship construction illustrates this remarkable increase in efficiency. With a 728-foot length, 78-foot beam, and 45-foot depth, Inland's new vessel had a maximum carrying capacity of 37,200 gross tons. Despite being 2 feet shorter than the *Ryerson*, the *Block*'s 3-foot wider beam and 6-foot greater depth combined with its boxy shape allowed it to carry 9,700 tons more cargo per trip than the Inland Steel fleet's previously most modern ship. As a self-unloader, the *Joseph L. Block* also spent less time in port than gearless bulk carriers of the same size. This allowed the motor vessel to maximize the number of voyages it completed during the shipping season. Built at a cost of $17 million, the *Joseph L. Block* increased the size of the

Inland Steel fleet back to seven vessels for a brief period while also raising its single trip carrying capacity to just over 140,000 gross tons, the highest it was ever to achieve.

In September of 1976, the *Clarence B. Randall* (2) laid up for the final time. Its career with the fleet at an end, Inland Steel sold the retired steamer to the Afram Brothers Company of Milwaukee, Wisconsin for non-transportation later that year. After languishing at that port for a number of years, the *Randall* made its one-way trip to the scrap yard in 1987 following failed attempts to convert the vessel into a floating dock and, later, a grain storage barge.

As is commonplace with most economic downturns, the recession of the mid-1970s took a heavy toll on the domestic steel industry as automobile sales fell and construction slowed. Burdened with overcapacity and facing stiff competition from cheap imported steel, Inland Steel placed a hold on the first phase of its expansion plans in 1977. Although 1978 proved a good year with profits amounting to $158.3 million, troubled times lay ahead for both the Inland Steel Company and the nation's steel industry as a whole. That same year, ore shipments on the lakes rebounded from the 67 million gross tons shipped in 1977 to reach 88.9 million gross tons.

During the late 1970s, Inland Steel's Caland Ore Company subsidiary began winding down its mining

Commissioned in 1976, the *Joseph L. Block* was the final ship constructed for the Inland Steel Company.
(Tom Salvner photo)

operation near Atikokan, Ontario. Although costs had risen over the years, the primary reason for the closure stemmed from the quality of the pellets produced by the operation. Prone to damage during transit and proving difficult to smelt, the chemical characteristics of these pellets resulted in higher costs for the steel making process in comparison to those from other sources. Unable to compete, Caland shipped its last railcar of pellets on April 30, 1980, nearly 20 years to the day of its inaugural shipment arriving at Indiana Harbor aboard the *John O. McKellar* (2).

While the Inland Steel Company never acquired a thousand-foot vessel of its own, the American Steamship Company built one such vessel to serve primarily in the delivery of taconite to the steelmaker's Indiana Harbor facility. Built in 1979 by the Bay Shipbuilding Corporation and appropriately named *Indiana Harbor*, this ship became American Steamship's second thousand-foot vessel constructed during that fleet's extensive modernization program of the 1970s and early 1980s. Christened on July 11, 1979 by Mignon Jaicks, wife of Inland Steel Chairman Frederick G. Jaicks, the *Indiana Harbor* departed on its maiden voyage on August 29 for Two Harbors, Minnesota to load a cargo of taconite destined for delivery to its namesake harbor.

With receipts totaling just over 92 million gross tons, the 1979 season saw that decade's heaviest movement of iron ore on the Great Lakes. Amounting to just 20,000 gross tons less than that shipped during the 1942 wartime season, this figure represents the fourth highest seasonal tonnage of that commodity ever shipped on the lakes. Despite the impressive statistics of the 1979 season and the 88.9 million gross tons of ore shipped during the preceding year, the nation stood on the precipice of another major economic recession. The resulting downturn in the domestic steel industry during the early years of the upcoming decade was to prove the most challenging to face the Great Lakes shipping industry since the dark years of the Great Depression.

Chapter Four
Sailing into Troubled Waters 1980-1998

At the beginning of the 1980 shipping season, the Inland Steel fleet stood at six vessels with a single trip carrying capacity of 129,000 gross tons. Ranging in age from the 72-year old *E. J. Block* to the modern *Joseph L. Block*, the fleet represented a microcosm of Great Lakes freighter design stretching back to the beginning of the twentieth century. With an average age of 39.2 years, the vessels in this fleet owed their longevity to the singular purpose of providing the Inland Steel Company with a dedicated method of transporting its raw materials.

Although the recession of the early 1980s had an adverse effect across the entire economic spectrum, it hit domestic steel producers particularly hard. Confronting falling demand and cheap imported steel during a time of financial uncertainty, production at the nation's steel mills slowed to a near standstill. The resulting drop in tonnage requirements sent several vessels to the wall due to a lack of cargoes, many of which never sailed again. Nowhere was this decline more noticeable than in the movement of iron ore on the Great Lakes/St. Lawrence Seaway system. Beginning in 1980 when 72,967,359 gross tons of ore moved across the waters of the lakes, this trade had fallen to only 38,512,574 gross tons in 1982, the lowest such level since the 1938 season. Despite rebounding somewhat the following year to 52,085,008 gross tons, the annual movement of ore on the Great Lakes never exceeded 61 million gross tons throughout the balance of the decade.

As the 1980s began, the last great period of U.S. flagged construction experienced thus far on the lakes entered its final phase. With the recent addition of a new class of efficient carriers and the modernization of several existing vessels coming at a time of plummeting demand, a significant downsizing of the U.S. fleet was an inevitable consequence of the poor economic conditions prevailing during the early part of the decade.

Its operational career at an end, the *Philip D. Block* laid up for the last time at Indiana Harbor on September 12, 1981. Seven weeks later, on October 30, another veteran of the Inland Steel fleet entered into a permanent layup when the *L. E. Block* tied up at Milwaukee, Wisconsin. Once one of the largest ships on the Great Lakes, the *L. E. Block*'s 15,900 gross ton carrying capacity was less than half that of its larger fleet mate, the *Joseph L. Block*, and only one-quarter of the 62,652 gross ton iron ore record established by the *Indiana Harbor* at Two Harbors, Minnesota on September 13, 1979.

Poor economic conditions prompted the sporadic

Operating in the twilight of its career, the *E. J. Block* departs the Soo Locks at Sault Ste. Marie, Michigan during the 1981 shipping season. (Tom Salvner photo)

temporary layups of the active vessels in the Inland Steel fleet in response to sluggish demand. Lacking self-unloading equipment, the *Edward L. Ryerson* was usually the first unit idled by fleet managers when cargoes became scarce. Benefiting from its conversion into a self-unloader, however, the *Wilfred Sykes* proved far more versatile in moving payloads outside those required by the steelmaker. As a result, fleet management frequently employed this steamer outside its traditional trade routes to serve a variety of customers located in ports on Lake

Michigan. Combined with the ore run between Escanaba and Indiana Harbor, such activities became so much a part of this ship's seasonal commitments that by the middle of the decade the *Wilfred Sykes* had become an uncommon visitor to the once familiar waters of Lake Superior.

Suffering terribly from the downturn in the steel industry during this period, the Inland Steel Company sustained losses amounting to $456 million between 1982 and 1985. Regardless of these financial challenges, however, the company pushed forward in its effort to improve productivity and develop new products. In addition to reducing its manufacturing capacity by 30-percent, Inland also divested itself of unprofitable ventures while at the same time expanding those proving more lucrative.

Following the retirement of the *Philip D. Block* and *L. E. Block*, the Inland Steel fleet's oldest and smallest ship, the *E. J. Block*, remained active in the transshipment of raw materials between the steel company's Dock #2 and Dock #3. Contrary to the prevailing trend towards larger vessels, the unique role in which the *E. J. Block* proved ideally suited allowed the 552-foot long vessel to survive long after the majority of its contemporaries had gone to the scrap yard. As it had for several years, this motor vessel took an occasional break from the Indiana Harbor ore shuttle for a run north on Lake Michigan to Escanaba, Michigan. The end finally came for the *E. J. Block* on August 4, 1984 when it entered an indefinite layup at Indiana Harbor. In 1986, the tug *Cindy B.* and a fleet of four barges assumed the transshipment role formerly performed by the *E. J. Block*.

In 1985, Inland Steel sold its long-idled *Philip D. Block* to Marine Salvage of Port Colborne, Ontario. Arriving at the scrap yard on November 14, the retired steamer remained at Port Colborne until its subsequent sale for scrapping overseas during the summer of 1986. Towed down the

A stern view of the *L. E. Block* heading towards Lake Superior at Sault Ste. Marie, Michigan in June of 1981, its final operational season. (Tom Salvner photo)

Atlantic Ocean in tandem with the *W. W. Holloway*, the *Philip D. Block* met that fate at Recife, Brazil later that year.

During the early to mid-1980s, the *Edward L. Ryerson* was laid up for short periods on numerous occasions due to fluctuating raw material demands. Beginning in the middle of the decade, however, this steamer entered into a pattern of prolonged periods of idleness followed by intermittent returns to service that have characterized its career to this very day. By the 1985 season, the drastic reduction of the Great Lakes shipping fleet during the previous five years had left the *Edward L. Ryerson* as one of only seven straight deck bulk carriers still operating under the American flag. These vessels consisted of Interlake Steamship's *J. L. Mauthe*, Rouge Steel's *Ernest R. Breech*, National Steel's *Paul H. Carnahan*, in addition to the Kinsman Line's *Kinsman Independent* (2), *Merle M. McCurdy*, and *William A. McGonagle*. Of these, only the *Edward L. Ryerson* and *Paul H. Carnahan* remained committed solely to the movement of iron ore for the steel industry, with the latter vessel ending its operational career in August of that year. Tying up at Indiana Harbor on December 11, 1985, the *Edward L. Ryerson* entered a layup lasting until March 26, 1988 when it departed the lower Lake Michigan port to load taconite pellets at Escanaba, Michigan.

In 1986, the Inland Steel Company downsized its

shipping fleet further when it sold the *L. E. Block* to Basic Marine, Inc. of Escanaba, Michigan for non-transportation use. Shortly following the sale, the tugs *Daryl C. Hannah* and *Carla Anne Selvick* towed the former Inland steamer to Escanaba. Towed down Lake Michigan the following summer, the *L. E. Block* arrived at South Chicago, Illinois on August 5, 1987 to begin a new career as a storage barge on Lake Calumet. Overloaded with cement and sinking into the muddy bottom early the following year, however, this vessel's use in such a role proved somewhat disappointing. Refloated with the removal of its storage cargo, the tug *Chippewa* returned the *L. E. Block* to Escanaba in October of 1988. Unused, the 621-foot long vessel remained at that city for nearly twenty years in a steadily deteriorating condition until its sale for scrapping in 2006. Towed from Escanaba on July 7, 2006 by the tug *Shannon*, the *L. E. Block* arrived at the International Marine Salvage scrap yard at Port Colborne, Ontario four days later for dismantling.

In May of 1987, the Inland Steel Company disposed of its last remaining retired vessel when it sold the *E. J. Block* to Marine Salvage for scrapping. Towed downbound past Detroit, Michigan on August 18, this elderly ship arrived at Port Colborne, Ontario two days later, where tugs secured it at the salvage company's scrap slip. Although commencing in January of 1988, scrapping of

The *Edward L. Ryerson* laid up at Sturgeon Bay, Wisconsin due to a lack of work. Since 1985, this ship has experienced several long-term periods of idleness. (Wendell Wilke photo)

the *E. J. Block* proved a protracted exercise lasting through the late months of 1991.

Reduced in size to three units by the sale of the *E. J. Block*, the Inland Steel fleet now consisted of the *Joseph L. Block, Edward L. Ryerson,* and *Wilfred Sykes.* Although the fleet's combined single trip carrying capacity had declined to 86,200 gross tons, its lowest level since 1959, this capability, in combination with cargoes carried by outside vessels, proved more than adequate for the steelmaker's requirements.

As the last gearless vessel in the fleet, the *Edward L. Ryerson* became a reserve unit during times of sluggish raw material demand. The possibility of this steamer receiving a self-unloading conversion similar to that given to the *Wilfred Sykes* has generated a considerable amount of speculation since the mid-1970s. In addition to economic considerations, however, the low cubic dimension configuration of this vessel's cargo hold arrangement has served to complicate such a project. Despite this matter receiving careful consideration, Inland Steel never financed a conversion and the *Edward L. Ryerson* remains a straight decker to this day.

The considerable downsizing of the Great Lakes fleet during the 1980s is reflected by the fact that at the beginning of the 1990 shipping season the U.S. flagged fleet consisted of 62 vessels engaged in the ore, coal, stone, and grain trades in comparison to the 133 such units in existence just ten years earlier. During this same time, the number of gearless bulk carriers in the fleet decreased from 80 to only 7 vessels. As can be expected, several shipping firms also met their demise during this turbulent period of Great Lakes history. Notable among these were the Cleveland Cliffs, Ford Motor Company, and National Steel fleets. Unsurprisingly given the contraction of the domestic steel industry, the United

States Steel Corporation saw its massive fleet shrink from 39 units in 1980 to just 11 in 1990.

Having endured the dark years of the early 1980s, Inland Steel returned to profitability during the later part of the decade. In 1987, the company entered into a partnership with the Japanese steel manufacturer Nippon Steel Corporation to construct a new $400 million cold rolling mill at New Carlisle, Indiana. Two years later, the steelmakers entered into a second partnership to build two galvanized coating lines at the same site. As the 1980s drew to a close, Inland Steel had grown to become the nation's fourth largest steel producer and its largest steel distributor. While losing $21 million in 1990, improving economic conditions leading into the middle of that decade generated a renewed demand in automobiles, a manufacturing sector in which the steelmaker was heavily involved. Increasing its global reach during this period, the company entered into a series of international partnerships with steel firms in China, India, and Mexico even as it continued to shutter unprofitable operations. These moves along with a recovering economy, allowed Inland Steel to generate a profit in 1994, its first since 1989.

In early 1994, the Inland Steel Company chartered the 680-foot *Adam E. Cornelius* (4) from the American Steamship Company. This agreement sidelined the

Edward L. Ryerson, which had ended its 1993 season at Sturgeon Bay, Wisconsin on January 24, 1994. Built by the American Ship Building Company's Toledo yard in 1973 as the *Roger M. Kyes,* this motor vessel has a carrying capacity of 28,200 gross tons at a draft of 28 feet 5 inches. Repainted in a derivative Inland Steel color scheme that did not include the company's billboard lettering, this vessel departed Toledo on May 5, 1994 to begin its first trip as part of the steelmaker's fleet.

Plagued by a number of accidents during its early

The *Adam E. Cornelius* (4) departing Toledo, Ohio on May 5, 1994 to begin its charter to the Inland Steel Company.
(James Hoffman photo)

career, the *Adam E. Cornelius* (4) suffered damage on at least two separate occasions during its time with the Inland Steel fleet. The first of these occurred early in its charter when it ran aground while approaching the upper entrance to the Poe Lock while downbound on the St. Marys River on July 14, 1994. Unloading a portion of its taconite cargo into the Interlake Steamship's *Elton Hoyt 2nd* (2) the following day, the *Cornelius* (4) broke free of the bottom with the assistance of two tugs before continuing to Indiana Harbor and then Sturgeon Bay, Wisconsin for repairs. A second mishap while in Inland colors took place in Lake Michigan on January 26, 1997, when ice damage caused considerable flooding in a forward compartment shortly after the vessel's departure from Escanaba, Michigan. As with the previous occurrence, repairs resulting from this incident took place at the Bay Shipbuilding yard at Sturgeon Bay.

Placed into dry dock at Sturgeon Bay in November of 1996 for its five-year survey and repainting, the *Edward L. Ryerson* returned to service on April 5, 1997 when it departed the shipyard to load taconite at Escanaba. Encountering boiler problems on the initial downbound voyage on Lake Michigan following its three-year layup, however, this steamer required a tow into Milwaukee the following day. With repairs completed, the *Ryerson* resumed its voyage to Indiana Harbor on April 9, 1997.

With the *Edward L. Ryerson*'s return to service, the Inland Steel fleet had four vessels in operation with a combined single trip carrying capacity of 114,400 gross tons. Not only was this the highest level of capacity operated by the fleet at any one time since 1981, it also represented the most vessels operating for the steelmaker since the 1984 season when the *E. J. Block* was retired.

In July of 1998, Ispat International N.V., a global steel producer headquartered in the Netherlands, completed its purchase of the Inland Steel Company in a deal worth approximately $1.4 billion. As the Jones Act, the federal law regulating shipping operations within the United States, prohibited foreign ownership of vessels trading between the nation's ports, this transaction necessitated the creation of two new companies. The first was the Indiana Harbor Steamship Co., which assumed ownership of the three ships in the Inland Steel fleet, while the second, Central Marine Logistics, Inc., was to manage the actual operation of the vessels. Soon afterwards, crews began removing all references to Inland Steel, including the billboard lettering, from the *Joseph L. Block*, *Edward L. Ryerson*, and *Wilfred Sykes*.

During the 1998 shipping season, the *Edward L. Ryerson* entered two short-term layups, the first between June and July, and the second between September and October of that year. Tying up for the winter at Sturgeon Bay on

December 12, 1998, this steamer was to remain idle for the next seven shipping seasons before a heavy demand for ore movement prompted its return to service on July 22, 2006. While the *Joseph L. Block* and *Wilfred Sykes* received new Ispat stack colors before the beginning of the 1999 shipping season, the *Ryerson* retained the Inland Steel markings on its unique stainless steel stack throughout this protracted layup period.

Its charter arrangement having concluded, the *Adam E. Cornelius* (4) returned to the American Steamship Company following the end of the 1998 shipping season. Repainted in that fleet's colors, this ship reentered service in April of the following year serving a variety of customers around the lakes. In years since, however, the *Adam E. Cornelius* (4) has been laid up on several occasions in response to a lack of available cargoes.

As of 2015, all three of the former Inland Steel vessels remain in existence. While the *Edward L. Ryerson* has been idle at Superior, Wisconsin since May 18, 2009, the *Joseph L. Block* and *Wilfred Sykes* continue to perform in the role that prompted their construction by regularly supplying raw materials to Indiana Harbor. In 2005, the former Inland Steel Company plant at that port changed hands once again when Ispat Inland merged with the International Steel Group (ISG) and LNM Holdings to become Mittal Steel USA. Just two years later, this firm was part of its parent company's merger with European steelmaker Arcelor to become the world's largest steel company, ArcelorMittal.

Between its formation in 1911 and dissolution in 1998, the Inland Steel fleet operated ten different vessels throughout its long history. With the exception of the canal-sized *The Inland* and the chartered *Adam E. Cornelius* (4), all of these ships enjoyed lengthy careers with the fleet. Remarkably, several of the older vessels in the fleet operated far longer than would have been possible if they had not been a component of the steelmaker's vertical integration policy of maintaining a dedicated method to transport raw materials into its Indiana Harbor facility. As one of the two ships acquired to form the fleet, the *W. R. Woodford* went on to serve a record 76 years with the Inland Steel Company first as the *N. F. Leopold* and later the *E. J. Block*. Thoroughly modernized and repowered in 1946, this vessel's ability to navigate the narrow bridge openings on the Indiana Harbor Ship Canal secured its future long into an era dominated by much larger ships.

Over the course of its history, the Inland Steel Company had four new ships built for its account. In chronological order, these were the *L. E. Block* (1927), *Wilfred Sykes* (1949), *Edward L. Ryerson* (1960), and *Joseph L. Block* (1976). Of these, the *L. E. Block* spent its entire operational career in Inland colors, while the three other vessels operated for the fleet until its dissolution to remain fleet mates today with Central Marine Logistics.

With its single purpose being the transportation of raw materials into its owner's sprawling steel making complex at Indiana Harbor, the Inland Steel fleet was destined to remain one of the smaller shipping firms on the Great Lakes despite a history of continuous improvement and the willingness to incorporate the latest advancements in new construction. This spirit of innovation and dedication has made this fleet one of the most memorable to ever operate on the inland seas.

Part Two

Individual Vessel Histories

Chapter Five
Steamer *Joseph Block*

In March of 1907, the American Ship Building Company experienced a widespread labor dispute when workers went on strike in its shipyards at Chicago, Cleveland, Lorain, Superior, and Wyandotte. This situation created the potential of serious delays in ship construction under contract at the affected yards. One such vessel was the Chicago yard's Hull #76 consigned to the Neptune Steamship Company, which was itself one of the many companies that made up the Hawgood fleet. The work stoppage prompted shipyard officials to transfer this work to another facility, which was not on strike. As such, this ship retained its Chicago yard hull number despite its construction actually taking place at the West Bay City Shipbuilding Company in West Bay City, Michigan.

Named *Arthur H. Hawgood* to honor one of the Hawgood brothers heavily involved in running the family's shipping operation, this ship first tasted water on October 5, 1907. In fact, the *Hawgood* was just one of three vessels launched on that date by the American Ship Building Company in three separate yards. The others included the steamer *Verona* at Lorain for the Lackawanna Steamship Company (Picklands, Mather & Co. managers) and the tug *Harvard* at Buffalo for the Great Lakes Towing Company.

Measuring 569 feet in length, 56 feet in beam, and with a 31-foot depth, the *Arthur H. Hawgood* had a carrying capacity of 10,800 gross tons. Propulsion incorporated a 1,900 indicated horsepower triple-expansion steam engine built at Cleveland by the American Ship Building Company. The engine received steam from two Scotch boilers manufactured by the Detroit Ship Building

A postcard view of the *Joseph Block* downbound in the MacArthur Lock during the mid-1960s. (Author's Collection)

Company with operating pressures of 170 psi each.

The *Arthur H. Hawgood* operated for the Neptune Steamship Company until its sale to the Inland Steel Company on September 1, 1911. This transaction came at a time when the Hawgood fleet was experiencing financial problems and just before the onset of some legal difficulties stemming from William A. and Arthur H. Hawgood having received secret kickbacks from the American Ship Building Company in connection to the construction of three ships. Merging all of their various fleets into the Acme Transit Company in 1911, the Hawgood family found it necessary to sell four of its ships to cover outstanding debts and expenses. Besides this steamer, the other units involved this downsizing included the *Henry A. Hawgood, William A. Hawgood,* and *W. R. Woodford.* Seizing the opportunity to acquire two relatively new vessels at bargain prices, Inland Steel also purchased the *W. R. Woodford.*

With no marine division of its own, Inland Steel contracted Hutchinson & Company of Cleveland to manage the two ships. This arrangement resulted in the two companies entering into a joint venture named the Inland Steamship Company, with Inland Steel being the major shareholder. To reflect its new ownership, the *Arthur H. Hawgood* was renamed *Joseph Block* in recognition of one of the steelmaker's principal founders prior to entering service at the beginning of the 1912 shipping season.

Although Hutchinson occasionally employed the *Joseph Block* to carry cargoes outside those consigned to Inland Steel, this ship's normal trading pattern concentrated on transporting ore, coal, and stone into its owner's steel making operation at Indiana Harbor, Indiana. During its early years in operation for the Inland Steamship Company, this ship was involved in a number of incidents.

Although there is no record of the *Joseph Block* sustaining any damage during the Great Storm of 1913, it nonetheless suffered at least two separate accidents that season. While downbound in the St. Marys River on August 15 of that year, the *Block* struck a pier as it prepared to pass through the Canadian lock at Sault Ste. Marie, Ontario. With the resulting hull damage proving minor in nature and above the waterline, this steamer was able to continue its trip before receiving permanent repairs during a subsequent dry docking. A more serious accident occurred a little more than two months later, on October 23, when the *Joseph Block* ran aground while departing Rogers City, Michigan. This occurred when the Bradley steamer *Calcite* struck the Inland vessel after its crew let go of its mooring lines at a dock on the opposite side of the slip. The contact between the two ships forced the bow of the *Joseph Block* to hit bottom with a force sufficient to damage a number of hull plates on its port side. In the resulting litigation, neither side admitted fault for the incident. Studying the factors involved, the arbitrator found the master of the *Joseph Block* at fault for not employing the services of a tug while departing Rogers City despite known problems associated with loaded vessels leaving the loading dock at that port. Possibly influenced by assertions of the *Block* having actually grounded before the two ships made contact, this ruling left the Inland Steamship Company little recourse but to pay for the damages.

While transiting Lake Superior in a spring storm on May 8, 1916, the *Joseph Block* was one of three steamers that came to the assistance of the steamer *S. R. Kirby* and its consort barge *George E. Hartnell*. Earlier that morning, the master of the *E. H. Utley* had become concerned for the welfare of the *S. R. Kirby* and its barge after observing the pair struggling in the turbulent waters of the lake near the Keweenaw Peninsula. When the *Kirby* broke in two and plunged to the bottom at around 11 o'clock that morning, the master of the *Utley* rushed his ship to location of the sinking. Unable to find any survivors, the *Utley* began pursuing the *Hartnell* in an effort to keep the barge from running ashore near Eagle Harbor, Michigan. Additional assistance soon arrived in the form of the *Joseph Block* and the 556-foot *Harry A. Berwind*, both of which began combing the lake for survivors. This effort resulted in the *Berwind* pulling the *Kirby*'s second mate, Joseph Mudray, from the cold waters of Lake Superior and the *Block*'s rescue of the lost steamer's fireman, Otto S. Lindquist. These two men proved to be the only survivors of the sinking that cost twenty lives.

While inbound to load iron ore at Superior, Wisconsin on May 14, 1917, the *Joseph Block* came upon a heavy ice pack extending approximately four miles into western Lake Superior. Arriving in port, a survey of the hull revealed some minor hull damage that required repairs following the end of the shipping season. On November 12, 1919, this ship once again experienced trouble on the largest of the five Great Lakes when it encountered a heavy fall storm while upbound in ballast to load ore at Superior. The severity of this gale proved sufficient to cause the *Joseph Block* to take on some water through leaking rivets and opened hull seams. A subsequent visit to a shipyard to remedy the stress of weather damage resulted in a $30,000 repair bill.

In 1936, ownership of the *Joseph Block* passed from the Inland Steamship Company to the Inland Steel Company. Following this transaction, Inland continued their vessel management agreement with Hutchinson & Company and the operation and trade routes of their vessels remained unaffected.

Consistent with a policy of modernizing its older vessels, Inland Steel invested in various upgrades to retain the *Joseph Block's* operational competiveness. These modifications included the installation of two new Babcock & Wilcox water tube boilers in 1941 along with new side tanks and tank tops in March of 1945. The latter project included the reconstruction of the vessel's spar deck with 17 single-piece hatches placed on 24-foot centers replacing the original telescoping hatches on 12-foot centers. In 1947, Inland undertook a further modernization program when it had the *Joseph Block's* boilers converted from coal to oil-fired.

During the early 1950s, the *Joseph Block*, along with the rest of Inland's steamers, received the distinctive fleet color scheme pioneered by the *Wilfred Sykes*. In 1957, Inland Steel assumed the management of this vessel after ending its longstanding arrangement with Hutchinson & Company. Although making frequent trips to Lake Superior during this timeframe, this ship remained heavily involved in the movement of iron ore between the Chicago & North Western ore dock at Escanaba and Indiana Harbor. It was during one such voyage that this ship nearly met its fate.

At 4:30 in the morning of May 22, 1968, the *Joseph Block* ran hard aground in the Porte des Morts (Death's Door)

Passage connecting Lake Michigan and Green Bay. This accident occurred while the steamer was en route to Escanaba to load a cargo consisting of 11,500 tons of taconite bound for Inland's blast furnaces. Despite the clear weather and with all of the appropriate navigational aids operating, the crew of the *Block* somehow allowed their vessel to stray outside the channel and strike the rocky bottom.

The United States Coast Guard responded to the grounding by dispatching a small boat from its Plum Island station and sending the cutter *Woodbine* to assist the stranded freighter. Additional help came from the tug *Arrow* belonging to the Roen Steamship Company of Sturgeon Bay, Wisconsin. Although the force of the stranding was sufficient to inflict severe hull damages to the *Joseph Block*, there were no injuries among its thirty-two crewmembers.

Using its own engine combined with a stern towline pulled by the *Arrow*, the *Joseph Block* broke free of its perch when it backed slowly off the rocky bottom at 4:30 that afternoon. After surveying the damage, the Coast Guard permitted the steamer to proceed to the Manitowoc Shipbuilding Company's yard at Manitowoc, Wisconsin, some 90 miles to the south. Following a cautious trip down Lake Michigan with a port list and accompanied by the cutter *Woodbine*, the *Joseph Block* arrived at the shipyard where it immediately entered the dry dock.

The full extent of the damages suffered in the grounding became apparent when shipyard workers drained the water from the dry dock. With some 100 bottom plates damaged by the grounding, the 61-year old steamer required extensive repairs before it could return to service. Having concluded that the cost of repairs represented an uneconomical proposition given the vessel's age, Inland Steel abandoned the *Joseph Block* to its underwriters a short time later.

While in most cases, such a decision usually results in a one-way trip to the scrap yard, the *Joseph Block* was to receive a new lease on life when Lake Shipping Inc. acquired it in June of 1968. A subsidiary of the American Ship Building Company, Lake Shipping had this steamer towed its owner's yard at South Chicago for repairs. Sold to Kinsman Marine Transit in June of the following year, this ship was renamed *George M. Steinbrenner* (2).

In its new fleet, this ship concentrated in the movement of grain, ore, and stone between U.S. ports on the upper lakes and those on the lower lakes. Despite the vast majority of these voyages ending without incident, the *George M. Steinbrenner* (2) ran into trouble on at least one occasion when it struck the Grassy Point railroad bridge while maneuvering in Duluth/Superior harbor on June 12,

1974.

Transferred to the S&E Shipping Corporation on August 21, 1975, this ship remained under Kinsman management. Departing from winter layup at Toledo on May 4, 1977, the *George M. Steinbrenner* (2) operated for just three months that season before returning to that port in August to be laid up for the final time. Sold for scrap the following year, the tugs *Wilfred M. Cohen* and *Princess No. 1* towed the *Steinbrenner* (2) down the Welland Canal and into the Dwor Metals yard at Ramey's Bend on August 25, 1978. During its scrapping, which began at the Marine Salvage yard at Port Colborne during the spring of 1979, a proposal to save the retired steamer's pilothouse as an observation platform at Lock 8 on the Welland Canal never came to fruition.

Chapter Six
Steamer *N. F. Leopold*

Acquired on September 1, 1911, the *W. R. Woodford* was one of two steamers purchased by Inland Steel from the Hawgood fleet to form the genesis of its own shipping fleet. The other vessel involved in this transaction was the previously described *Arthur H. Hawgood*. As such, Inland placed both of these ships into the newly formed Inland Steamship Company and under the management of Hutchinson & Company. Prior to entering service during the 1912 shipping season, the *W. R. Woodford* was renamed *N. F. Leopold*.

Built at a cost of $430,000 by the West Bay City Shipbuilding Company at West Bay City, Michigan in 1908, the *W. R. Woodford* proved to be the final new vessel acquired by the Hawgood fleet. This 552-foot freighter's original powerplant consisted of a 1,765 indicated horsepower triple-expansion steam engine built by the Detroit Shipbuilding Company.

Following its purchase by Inland Steel, the *N. F. Leopold* became committed to the supply of raw materials to that firm's steel producing facility at Indiana Harbor. During the early years of its new career, this vessel was involved in at least two minor incidents. On April 28, 1915, the *N. F. Leopold* touched bottom as it was arriving at Rogers City, Michigan. Despite the grounding, the *Leopold* was able to load its stone cargo for delivery to Indiana Harbor prior to being dry docked at South Chicago for permanent repairs. Just two years later, on May 3, 1917, this steamer suffered some hull damage while transiting an ice field in Lake Superior at a location approximately 15 miles north of Whitefish Point. A visit to a shipyard to rectify this damage resulted in a $10,000 repair bill.

A potentially more serious accident took place on May 1, 1924 when the *N. F. Leopold* collided with the Pioneer Steamship Company's *Charles L. Hutchinson* (1) in the upper St. Marys River. Interestingly, Hutchinson & Company managed both of these bulk freighters. With the *Leopold* downbound with ore and the *Hutchinson* upbound in ballast this accident occurred as both vessels met in clear, but windy, conditions at 3:30 in morning after exchanging passing whistle signals. While passing, the bow of the *N. F. Leopold* suddenly swung into the port side of the *Charles L. Hutchinson* (1) to connect in a glancing blow that inflicted minor damage to both ships. Subsequent arbitration found both vessels equally at fault for the accident, thereby holding each owner 50% liable for the cost of repairs.

Two accidents befell this ship during the 1928 navigation

The *E. J. Block* upbound on the St. Marys River.
(Author's Collection)

season. The first came on April 16, 1928 when the *N. F. Leopold* touched bottom near Poe's Reef in Lake Michigan. Although the *Leopold* was able to continue its trip to Indiana Harbor, a subsequent survey revealed 15 damaged hull plates. A further incident on August 22 of that year resulted in the Inland steamer losing one of its propeller blades after hitting an underwater obstruction at Indiana Harbor.

As with the *Joseph Block* and *L. E. Block*, Inland Steel assumed direct ownership of the *N. F. Leopold* from the Inland Steamship Company in 1936. On November 1 of that same year, this ship encountered a heavy storm on Lake Michigan while on a trip from Port Inland, Michigan to Indiana Harbor with a cargo of limestone. With its pilothouse and forward cabins severely damaged, the *Leopold* managed to make port with storm damage amounting to a $35,000 repair bill.

Renaming this ship *E. J. Block* in 1943, the Inland Steel Company sent this vessel to the American Ship Building Company's Lorain yard three years later to receive an extensive refit that enabled it to operate for nearly another forty years. This major reconstruction project included the replacement of the *Block*'s original triple-expansion steam engine with two General Motors/ Westinghouse 1,424 brake horsepower diesel-electric engines. As the first of its kind performed upon a lake freighter, this conversion garnered considerable attention within the Great Lakes shipping community. While at the shipyard, workers also replaced the original telescoping hatches on 12-foot centers with hatches fitted with single-piece covers on 24-foot centers and the associated traveling hatch crane. Further improvements included the installation of new stern cabins and an improved steering gear. Benefiting from a technology that matured during the World War II, the *E. J. Block* also received a radar set, thereby becoming one of the first commercial vessels on the Great Lakes fitted with this major advancement in navigational equipment.

As the project neared its conclusion, an accident aboard the *E. J. Block* resulted in the death of one shipyard worker. This occurred on September 8, 1946, when Paul Kerecz, an electrician from Amherst, Ohio was electrocuted during the installation of a new switchboard panel. Just ten days later, the motor vessel sailed out of Lorain to begin sea trials with its new powerplant.

Returning to its role of supplying raw materials to Inland Steel's plant at Indiana Harbor, the *E. J. Block* had its diesel-electric engines rebuilt in 1949. Repainted in Inland's new fleet colors a short time later, this ship remained under Hutchinson & Company management until Inland assumed that role outright in 1957. Three years later, the *E. J. Block* struck bottom while downbound in the St. Marys River. After unloading its cargo at Indiana Harbor, the *Block* proceeded to Manitowoc for repairs. Continuing a practice of upgrading its older vessels, Inland Steel had the *Block* fitted with a bow thruster during the early 1960s.

On August 1, 1970, the *E. J. Block*'s troubles in the St. Marys River continued when it ran aground at Johnson Point. This incident required the 62-year old vessel to pay a visit to the Fraser Shipyards at Superior, Wisconsin for repairs to 36 hull plates at a cost of nearly $250,000. At the beginning of the 1971 shipping season, Inland Steel placed the *E. J. Block* on a temporary route that saw it carrying steel coils between Indiana Harbor and Milwaukee, a sailing distance of approximately 100 miles. Departing its homeport to conduct the first of these voyages on March 23, this vessel had delivered three such cargoes to the Wisconsin port by April 3 of that year.

By the mid-1970s, the *E. J. Block* and *Clarence B. Randall* (2) represented the two smallest ships in the Inland Steel fleet. As such, these vessels had been far surpassed in terms of both size and carrying capacity compared to more modern fleet units such as the *Wilfred Sykes*, *Edward L. Ryerson*, and the newly built *Joseph L. Block*. The latter vessel could in fact carry cargoes over three times larger than the *E. J. Block*'s modest 11,500 gross ton carrying capacity while also being able to unload without the use of shore side equipment. While the construction of the *Joseph L. Block* in 1976 directly led to Inland Steel retiring the *Clarence B. Randall* (2), the small size of the *E. J. Block* enabled it to survive, at least temporarily, in an age of increasingly larger ships by its ability to pass through narrow railway bridges crossing the Indiana Harbor Ship Canal. Therefore, this ship was destined to serve out the remainder of its career primarily shuttling raw materials between Inland Steel's docks #2 and #3, with an occasional run up Lake Michigan to load ore at Escanaba and even rarer voyages into Lake Superior.

The *E. J. Block* operated until laying up for the final time at Indiana Harbor on August 4, 1984. The factors influencing this decision included the vessel's age and an inability to compete during a time of a recession in the steel industry. Furthermore, in 1986 Inland Steel inaugurated the use of the tug *Cindy B.* and a fleet of four barges to move raw materials between its docks requiring passage through the narrow bridges. The retired motor vessel remained idle at Indiana Harbor until its sale to Marine Salvage for scrapping in May of 1987. Towed to its final destination by the tugs *Glenada* and *Tusker*, the *E. J. Block* arrived at Ramey's Bend on August 20, 1987. Although work began in January of the following year, the dismantling of this ship proved a long affair as it was not completed until 1991. With its career with Inland Steel stretching 76 years, the *E. J. Block* holds the longevity record of any vessel to serve as a member of the steelmaker's shipping fleet.

Chapter Seven
Steamer *L. E. Block*

In 1927, the Inland Steamship Company commissioned its first newly built bulk freighter when it placed the steamer *L. E. Block* into service. Named for the chairman of Inland Steel's board of directors, this ship was built at Lorain, Ohio by the American Ship Building Company. Christened by the daughter of its namesake, Babette Block, this ship slid off its building ways and into the wintry waters of the Black River on February 1, 1927. With the fitting out process completed over the following two months, the *L. E. Block* began its maiden voyage on April 14 of that year when it departed Toledo, Ohio with a cargo of coal destined for delivery to Indiana Harbor.

With a length of 621 feet, a 64-foot beam, and a 33-foot depth, the *L. E. Block* was one of the largest ships on the Great Lakes when it entered service. This ship was generally similar to the *Harry Coulby* (2) built by the American Ship Building that same year for the Interlake Steamship Company but one foot narrower in beam and ten feet shorter in length. Powered by a 2,500 shaft horsepower triple-expansion steam engine, the *L. E. Block* soon settled into a pattern of carrying raw materials into

Indiana Harbor to facilitate its owner's manufacturing operation. Operated under the management of Hutchinson & Company, however, this ship occasionally operated on trade routes outside of those dictated by the requirements of Inland Steel.

While the *L. E. Block* was destined to enjoy a relatively quiet career in terms of accidents, it did suffer at least one incident of note during its time in the Inland Steamship Company. After loading a cargo of iron ore at Escanaba,

A 1977 view of the *L. E. Block* upbound in the MacArthur Lock at Sault Ste. Marie, Michigan while on a voyage to load a cargo of iron ore on Lake Superior. (Author's Collection)

Michigan on the afternoon of October 29, 1933, the *Block* ran aground as it backed away from the loading dock in preparation to set sail for Indiana Harbor. Damaging a number of hull plates and opening up some seams, the grounding resulted in repairs totaling just over $19,000.

Brought under direct ownership of Inland Steel in 1936 with the vessel auction associated with the dissolution of the Inland Steamship Company, the *L. E. Block*, like the other vessels belonging to the steelmaker's fleet, remained under the management of Hutchinson & Company.

A giant for its day, the *L. E. Block* established a number of cargo records during its early years of operation. These included four separate records for the carriage of iron ore from Lake Superior ports during a three-year period stretching between the summers of 1936 and 1939. The first such cargo consisted of 14,651 gross tons of ore loaded at Superior, Wisconsin on July 13, 1936. On June 14 of the following year, the *Block* surpassed this benchmark when it returned to that same port to load a record 15,564 gross tons of ore. Another record cargo came aboard on August 2, 1938 when the Inland steamer loaded 15,726 gross tons of ore at Marquette, Michigan, which it later surpassed by a small margin nearly one year later by loading a 15,778 gross ton cargo of the steel making mineral at Superior. Unsurprisingly given the *L.*

E. *Block*'s normal trading pattern, all four of these record cargoes were destined for Indiana Harbor.

The *L. E. Block* was by no means alone in the quest to establish new benchmarks in cargo carriage records on the Great Lakes during this period. The *Block*'s primary competitors in this field consisted of Interlake's *Harry Coulby* (2) and the *Lemoyne* (1) of the Canada Steamship Lines. Although larger ships appeared during the mid-1940s in the form of the Pittsburgh Steamship Company's "Super" class, the pattern of cargo records established by this trio of vessels was not surpassed by a wide margin until Inland Steel placed the *Wilfred Sykes* into service during April of 1950.

During the late 1940s, Inland Steel embarked upon a period of fleet improvement programs designed to modernize its aging fleet. Although the reconstruction and diesel-electric conversion of the *E. J. Block* represented the most ambitious of these projects, the steelmaker also repowered two of its steamers during the early 1950s. In 1953, the *L. E. Block*'s original triple-expansion steam engine and three Scotch boilers were replaced by a new 4,950 shaft horsepower Westinghouse Electric steam turbine and two Babcock & Wilcox oil-fired boilers. In addition to the adoption of new fleet colors, the 1950s also witnessed Inland Steel terminating its long-term vessel management arrangement with Hutchinson

The *L. E. Block* steaming upbound in the St. Marys River on
August 1, 1981. (Tom Salvner photo)

& Company when it began managing its own fleet
operations at the end of 1956.

The *L. E. Block* remained the largest ship in the Inland
Steel fleet until the revolutionary *Wilfred Sykes* entered
service in 1950. By 1960, this steamer had fallen to third
place in terms of single trip carrying capacity within the
fleet following the commissioning of the *Edward L.
Ryerson*. In fact, the 15,900 gross ton carrying capacity of
the *L. E. Block* was only 900 tons greater than that of the
older *Philip D. Block* following that vessel's 1951

lengthening from 600 to 672 feet. Although making frequent visits to Escanaba, the *L. E. Block* remained heavily committed to the movement of iron ore from the Lake Superior region to Indiana Harbor during this timeframe, and in fact, throughout the balance of its operational career. Lake Superior loading ports visited by this steamer included Marquette, Superior, and Port Arthur (later Thunder Bay), Ontario.

On July 28, 1971, the *L. E. Block* arrived at Manitowoc to receive new side tanks and tank tops along with new ballast piping as part of a three-month project costing approximately $500,000. Two years later, on August 13, 1973, this steamer ran aground in the St. Marys River. The *Block* sailed for two more seasons until the Bay Shipbuilding Corporation repaired the damage from this grounding during the ship's 1975-1976 winter layup at Sturgeon Bay, Wisconsin.

While at Thunder Bay to load ore on July 27, 1979, the *L. E. Block* collided with the tug *George N. Carleton*. Proving minor in nature, this incident inflicted insignificant damage to both vessels.

As its career drew to a close, the *L. E. Block* made a few rare trips into Lake Erie carrying iron ore. These voyages included a trip into Cleveland, Ohio in June of 1978, during which it ventured up the twisting Cuyahoga River and a subsequent visit to Conneaut on June 24, 1981.

Outclassed by larger ships and with the onset of a major recession in the domestic steel industry, the *L. E. Block* laid up for the final time as an operational carrier at Milwaukee, Wisconsin on October 30, 1981.

Purchased by Basic Marine, Inc. in 1986, the tugs *Daryl C. Hannah* and *Carla Anne Selvick* towed the *L. E. Block* into Escanaba on November 11 of that year. Towed down Lake Michigan the following year, the retired steamer arrived at South Chicago on August 5, 1987 for use a as cement storage barge on Lake Calumet. The *Block*'s career

Retired from active service, the *L. E. Block* languishes at Escanaba, Michigan during the 1990s.
(James Hoffman photo)

in this role proved short-lived, however, as by early 1988 crews had overloaded it with cement. This caused the hull to sink some four feet into the soft bottom of Lake Calumet, a situation not fully rectified until the final removal of the cement cargo in September of that same year.

At 8:30 in the morning of October 12, 1988, the tug *Chippewa*, with the assistance of the tug *Eddie B.*, pulled the *L. E. Block* away from its dock on Lake Calumet to begin its return voyage to Escanaba. Delayed by high winds, the tow spent the night anchored inside the breakwall before venturing into Lake Michigan the following day. Arriving back at Escanaba, the *L. E. Block* was tied up at the Basic Marine yard near downtown, where it was to remain for nearly eighteen years.

Slowly rusting away, the retired Inland Steel steamer eventually roused the ire of those in the community that objected to its deteriorating condition as the years passed by. The conflict between the vessel's owners and the city finally came to a head during the summer of 2006 and resulted in Basic Marine selling the *L. E. Block* to International Marine Salvage of Port Colborne, Ontario for scrapping in June of that year.

During the early morning hours of July 7, 2006, Gaelic Tugboat Company's *Shannon* towed the *L. E. Block* from its long term berth to begin the 680 mile voyage to the scrap yard. With its Inland Steel fleet markings faded and peeling, but still recognizable, the *L. E. Block* passed slowly down the St. Clair and Detroit rivers two days later as the scrap tow continued towards its destination. Arriving at the eastern end of Lake Erie, the *Shannon* delivered the *L. E. Block* to the Port Colborne scrap dock on July 11, 2006 with the assistance of the tugs *Charlie E.*, *Sea Hound*, and *Vac*. By December of the following year, workers at the scrap yard had completed dismantling the veteran carrier.

Chapter Eight
Steamer *Philip D. Block*

First entering water at the American Ship Building Company yard at Lorain, Ohio on January 17, 1925, the steamer *Philip D. Block* became the first ship launched at that city since a tornado demolished the shipyard on June 28 of the previous year. Built for the Pioneer Steamship Company of Cleveland, Mrs. Henry D. Strauss christened this 600-foot vessel at five minutes past noon on that winter day. Operating under the management of Hutchinson & Company, the *Philip D. Block* began its maiden voyage on April 11, 1925 when it departed Huron, Ohio with a cargo of coal destined for delivery to Indiana Harbor.

Named for the second son of Joseph Block who joined his father to form the Inland Steel Company in 1893, the *Philip D. Block* spent much of its season committed to the transport of raw materials into Indiana Harbor. In its original configuration, this steamer's propulsion consisted of a 2,200 shaft horsepower triple-expansion steam engine and three Scotch boilers each of which measured 13 feet 6 inches in diameter and 11 feet in length.

The *Philip D. Block* in its final configuration following a pair of major reconstruction projects during the early 1950s.
(Author's Collection)

The *Philip D. Block* continued operating for the Pioneer Steamship Company until its sale to Inland Steel in April of 1936. This transaction came at the same time the steelmaker moved to bring the *Joseph Block, L. E. Block,* and *N. F. Leopold* into its corporate structure through the dissolution of the Inland Steamship Company partnership with Hutchinson & Company. Having already been committed to providing Inland Steel with its raw material transportation needs and remaining under Hutchinson management, this corporate restructuring had no effect upon the *Philip D. Block's* established trading patterns.

At the end of the 1950 shipping season, Inland Steel sent the *Philip D. Block* to the American Ship Building Company's yard at South Chicago, Illinois to undergo a major reconstruction. The most significant feature of this project was the insertion of a 72-foot midsection that brought this steamer's overall length to 672 feet and raised its carrying capacity to 15,000 gross tons. In fact, the lengthening resulted in the *Philip D. Block* growing to become just 6 feet shorter than the *Wilfred Sykes*, which, at the time, was the longest ship on the Great Lakes. In addition to new side tanks and tank tops, the reconstruction also included the installation of a new, and larger, pilothouse incorporating a modernistic style similar to that of the *Sykes*.

Its reconstruction completed, the *Philip D. Block* began its maiden trip in its newly lengthened state when it departed from Indiana Harbor on the evening of April 30, 1951. Bound for Superior to load iron ore, the steamer proceeded slowly up Lake Michigan to allow its crew time to test out the newly installed equipment and navigational instruments.

At the conclusion of the 1952 season, the *Philip D. Block* returned to the American Ship Building Company's South Chicago yard to have its triple-expansion engine replaced by a 4,950 shaft horsepower Westinghouse Electric steam turbine. This repowering project also included the replacement of the ship's three coal-fired Scotch boilers with two oil-fired Babcock & Wilcox water tube boilers. While at the shipyard, workers also installed a new tail shaft and rebuilt the *Block*'s stern cabins.

Throughout a career spanning some sixty years, the *Philip D. Block* managed to survive its long tenure on the Great Lakes without suffering any significant accidents. Nonetheless, this ship is known to have been involved in one minor incident while docked at Indiana Harbor. This occurred on May 24, 1955, when the Pioneer Steamship

A stern view of the *Philip D. Block* upbound on the St. Marys River during the 1975 shipping season. (Tom Salvner photo)

Company's *G. A. Tomlinson* (1) was departing from Inland Steel's Dock #2. Having left the dock, the *Tomlinson* was maneuvering in the channel with the aid of a tug in preparation to depart the harbor when a gust of wind forced its stern into the side of the *Philip D. Block*, which was moored directly astern of the dock space vacated by the Pioneer steamer. Although the *G. A. Tomlinson* (1) required some minor hull repairs, this incident inflicted only superficial damage to the Inland steamer.

By the late 1960s, the before mentioned lengthening and subsequent load line revisions had given the *Philip D. Block* a 15,400 gross ton carrying capacity at its 22 foot 1 inch mid-summer draft restriction. This enabled the *Block* to achieve some respectable seasonal tonnage statistics compared to many of its contemporaries. This was particularly true when this ship operated for extended periods on the Indiana Harbor-Escanaba run. Encompassing a round trip distance of just under 600 miles, this route across the length of Lake Michigan did not involve any of the congested river passages and lock transits necessary on the much longer trips to load ore on Lake Superior. In 1964, the *Philip D. Block* carried over one-million tons in a single season for the first time in its career, a feat made largely possible by loading the majority of its seventy-four ore cargoes at Escanaba.

Nearing the end of its operational life during the 1970s,

The *Philip D. Block* at the Marine Salvage scrap yard at Port Colborne, Ontario prior to its resale for scrapping overseas. To the right, the hull of the *Hudson Transport* sits prior to its conversion to the barge *Scurry*. (James Hoffman photo)

the *Philip D. Block* spent much of that decade trading on Lake Michigan, the monotony of this trade route broken only by an occasional trip to Lake Superior to load ore at Thunder Bay or Superior. As the Great Lakes shipping industry entered into a period of decline during the early 1980s, this steamer became a victim of this downsizing when it laid it up for the final time at Indiana Harbor on September 12, 1981.

The *Philip D. Block* remained at Inland Steel's homeport

until its sale in 1985 to Marine Salvage of Port Colborne, Ontario. Having departed Indiana Harbor for the final time, the retired steamer arrived at Port Colborne on November 14 when the tug *Ohio*, with the assistance of the tugs *Glenevis* and *Lac Manitoba*, maneuvered the *Block* into the scrap berth at Ramey's Bend. Following its arrival at the scrap yard, workers cut a hole into the front of the pilothouse to remove its navigational equipment. For the most part, however, the *Philip D. Block* remained relatively untouched at Port Colborne until Marine Salvage resold the vessel for scrapping overseas in mid-1986.

Towed by the tugs *Glenevis*, *Salvage Monarch*, and *Stormont*, the *Philip D. Block* passed down the Welland Canal on August 22, 1986 bound for Quebec City. Arriving at its destination, the *Block* was paired with the ex-Columbia Transportation (Oglebay Norton) self-unloader *W. W. Holloway* in preparation for a tandem tow by the Polish tug *Jantar* down the Atlantic to Brazil. Departing Quebec City on September 16, 1986, the *Jantar* towed the two retired steamers into Recife, Brazil on October 24, where scrapping of the *Philip D. Block* began a short time later.

Chapter Nine
Motor Vessel *The Inland*

Of the ten vessels operated by Inland Steel during its long history of fleet operations, none had a length of service as short as that of the motor vessel *The Inland*. This ship came into the fleet in April of 1946, when Hutchinson & Company purchased it from the American Steel and Wire Company while acting as an agent for the Inland Steel Company. With dimensions allowing it to transit the pre-Seaway locks and thus operate in both Great Lakes and saltwater trades, this crane equipped vessel stood in stark contrast to the bulk freighters operated by Inland Steel to supply its raw material transportation needs. Such traits, however, were the exact reason as to why this ship came into the fleet as its acquisition was part of the steelmaker's strategy to gain a favorable position in negotiating freight rates for its finished products.

Built in 1926 by the Federal Shipbuilding and Dry Dock Company at Kearney, New Jersey, this ship was launched as the *Steel Chemist* for the United States Steel Products Company, which was itself a division of the massive United States Steel Corporation. With an overall length of 258 feet 3 inches, this ship's design allowed it to

The Inland underway during its brief service for the Inland Steel Company.
(Thro Collection, University of Wisconsin – Superior)

operate in delivering steel products to various ports on the Great Lakes and the East Coast. The *Steel Chemist*, was in fact, one of four such vessels commissioned by the United States Steel Products Company for this purpose. Constructed by the same shipyard using a shared design, the other units included the *Steelmotor*, *Steelvendor*, and *Steel Electrician*.

Powered by a 950 brake horsepower diesel engine built

by the Worthington Pump & Machinery Corporation of Buffalo, New York, the *Steel Chemist* spent most of the Second World War trading on the East Coast. Acting for the Inland Steel Company, Hutchinson & Company purchased the *Steel Chemist* on April 18, 1946. Immediately following this transaction, Inland Steel renamed this ship *The Inland*. Equipped with two deck-mounted cranes, this motor vessel was capable of handling up to 2,900 gross tons of steel products in its two cargo holds.

Acquired for the before stated purpose of influencing freight rate negotiations, *The Inland* had a very brief career in the Inland Steel fleet during which it operated without incident. Becoming no longer required, the steelmaker sold *The Inland* to Transit Tankers & Terminals Ltd. of Montreal, Quebec in May of 1948.

Following its purchase, the new owners of this ship sent it to St. Catharines, Ontario for conversion into a tanker at the Port Weller Dry Docks. Renamed *Transinland*, this ship entered service in the liquid bulk trade in May of 1949. In 1954, a repowering resulted in the installation of a 1,600 brake horsepower Fairbanks Morse diesel engine that dated back to 1944. Although ownership of this motor vessel transferred to Coastlake Tankers Ltd. in 1953 and to Canadian Sealakers Ltd. in 1965, the *Transinland* remained under Transit Tankers & Terminals Ltd.

management.

By the mid-1960s, many of the ships in this fleet had entered into periods of extended idleness as newer tankers entered service on the Great Lakes and St. Lawrence Seaway. In October of 1968, the Hall Corporation of Canada acquired the *Transinland*, which it renamed *Inland Transport*. In addition, Hall also purchased the *Coastal Carrier* and *Coastal Creek*, which became the *Bay Transport* (2) and *Creek Transport* respectively. The purpose of these acquisitions was to secure some short-term tanker capacity pending the delivery of new tankers Hall had under construction at the time. As such, all three of these ships had relatively short careers in their new fleet. The *Inland Transport*, however, served longer than originally intended due to an increased tanker demand Hall Corporation experienced during the early 1970s. Incorporating four separate liquid cargo tanks, the final configuration of this vessel provided a carrying capacity of 25,000 barrels at its 17 foot 1 inch mid-summer draft.

Despite having a quiet operational career in terms of accidents, the *Inland Transport*'s luck finally ran out on November 4, 1972 when it ran aground at Little Current, Ontario. Released from its stranding in Georgian Bay with heavy hull damages, the *Inland Transport* went into indefinite layup at Sarnia, Ontario. While laid up at that port, vandals inflicted a considerable amount of harm to this vessel in the form of broken windows and serious damage to its internal structure. Purchased by Harry Gamble Shipyards after spending nearly four years idle, the *Inland Transport* left Sarnia under tow on July 5, 1976 bound for Port Dover, Ontario, where it remained until its subsequent scrapping at Port Maitland, Ontario in 1980.

Chapter Ten
Steamer *Wilfred Sykes*

In 1948, the Inland Steel Company awarded the American Ship Building Company a contract to construct the first U.S. flagged Great Lakes bulk freighter to enter service following the end of World War II. With a 678-foot length, 70-foot beam, and a 37-foot depth, this vessel was to be the largest ever built up to that time for service on the lakes. It was also the first to feature a carrying capacity in excess of 20,000 gross tons. Inland Steel's announcement of its intention to build this carrier in June of 1948 generated considerable excitement throughout the Great Lakes shipping community. Two months later, the steelmaker released a statement announcing that its new ship, the construction of which was to take place at American Ship Building's Lorain, Ohio yard, was to be named *Wilfred Sykes* in honor of the company's then current president.

Without ceremony, shipyard workers laid the keel plate for the *Wilfred Sykes* on November 1, 1948. Utilizing prefabrication techniques wherever possible, work progressed quickly as the vessel took shape over the next eight months. On the morning of June 28, 1949, a large crowd began gathering at the American Ship Building Company's Lorain yard to witness the launching of Inland Steel's giant new vessel. At 11:30 that morning, Mrs. Wilfred Sykes smashed the traditional bottle of champagne against the bow of her husband's namesake. The crack of the bottle signaled the release of ten guillotines that severed a like number of 8-inch hawsers that were holding the ship on its building ways. Free of its restraints, the *Wilfred Sykes* began a slow inexorable slide towards an adjacent flooded dry dock only 120 feet wide that was to serve as a launching slip. Within seconds, the steel freighter entered its element with a giant splash that pushed a wave of water littered with shattered timbers against the opposite side of the slip.

The innovative design of this ship included several features that were to influence shipbuilding practices throughout the 1950s. With the aft deckhouse stretching completely across its beam, Inland Steel's new steamer featured an enclosed stern. This design permitted the inclusion of internal passageways that allowed access to each individual room without requiring the crew to venture outside as was the case in previous vessels. In contrast to the tall stovepipe shaped smokestacks installed on most steel lake freighters up to this time, the design of the *Wilfred Sykes* incorporated a shorter stack with a streamlined casing. While retaining a profile in common with traditional freshwater shipbuilding practices, the forward cabins featured a much larger pilothouse than those installed on earlier vessels.

In addition to its modernistic appearance, Inland Steel also gave the *Wilfred Sykes* one of the most distinctive color schemes ever applied to a Great Lakes freighter. This consisted of a dark brown hull with a white stripe running completely around the vessel just a few feet below the level of the spar deck. The forecastle and stern featured white, gray, and dark blue bands with the

A photograph of the *Wilfred Sykes* loading iron ore on its first trip to Marquette, Michigan on May 12, 1950.
(Author's Collection)

steamer's name in black lettering. While the white fore and aft cabins featured gray bands, the pilothouse received only a dark blue band running just below its windows that extended to wrap around the top of the captain's quarters and office. On each side of the hull, large white billboard lettering spelled out "INLAND STEEL" with the steelmaker's diamond logo centered between "INLAND" and "STEEL." Incorporating a white base, the stack featured a large red Inland Steel diamond logo centered upon a wide band of stainless steel. Directly above and below the strip of stainless steel was a red and dark blue band respectively. Shortly after the *Wilfred Sykes* entered service, Inland Steel applied this unique color scheme to the balance of its fleet.

Powered by a 7,000 shaft horsepower Westinghouse Electric steam turbine, the *Wilfred Sykes* conducted its sea trials in Lake Erie on November 28, 1949, during which it achieved a top speed of 17.44 mph despite a 30 mph headwind. Following a series of adjustments, the *Sykes* ventured back into Lake Erie on December 13 for a second set of sea trials. With final work stretching throughout the balance of the year, Inland Steel accepted delivery of its new steamer on January 12, 1950.

After signing the contract with American Ship Building, Inland Steel assigned Captain Howard H. Kizer to serve as its representative at the shipyard. Slated to command the *Wilfred Sykes* when it entered service during the 1950 shipping season, Kizer became intimately involved with the ship as it emerged from a pile of steel plates and fittings at the Lorain shipyard. When Howard Kizer became seriously ill in early 1950, however, Inland Steel appointed another of its senior captains, George W. Fisher, to command the *Wilfred Sykes* when it entered service that spring. Captain Kizer subsequently passed away that November just a few weeks short of one year after commanding the *Sykes* during its sea trials.

Amid considerable fanfare, the *Wilfred Sykes* departed Lorain on April 19, 1950 bound for Toledo, Ohio to load a cargo of coal destined for Indiana Harbor, Indiana on its maiden voyage. Personifying the newest addition to the Great Lakes shipping fleet as "Queen of the Lakes," newspapers across the nation reported the progress of the revolutionary carrier as it made its way up the lakes. Greeted by a large crowd, the *Wilfred Sykes* sailed into Indiana Harbor on April 26 to conclude its maiden voyage. Speaking about the carrying capacity and speed capabilities of the new steamer, Edward L. Ryerson, chairman of Inland Steel, proudly informed members of the press in attendance at the gathering that the *Sykes* would "handle the tonnage of two lesser ships."

Like the other ships owned by the Inland Steel Company at the time, the *Wilfred Sykes* was managed by Hutchinson

& Company when it entered service. This arrangement lasted until Inland began managing its own fleet operations following the end of the 1956 shipping season.

As the largest ship on the Great Lakes until the *Joseph H. Thompson* entered service in 1952, it is unsurprising that the *Wilfred Sykes* established a number of cargo records during its early career. Between September 7, 1950 and August 27, 1952, this ship set five separate cargo records ranging from 19,120 to 21,223 gross tons of iron ore. All of these records cargoes were loaded at Superior, Wisconsin and unloaded at Inland Steel's complex at Indiana Harbor.

On the morning of May 11, 1953, the *Wilfred Sykes* was one of seven vessels to respond to a distress call from the steamer *Henry Steinbrenner* (1) when it foundered during a spring storm in western Lake Superior. Battling 70 mph winds, other lake steamers rushing to the scene included Hanna's *Joseph H. Thompson*, Paterson's *Ontadoc* (1), and the *Hochelaga* of the Canada Steamship Lines. Rounding out the initial search for survivors were the *D. M. Clemson* (2), *William E. Corey*, and *D. G. Kerr* (2), all of which belonged to the massive United States Steel Corporation fleet. Arriving on the scene at about the same time as the *Joseph H. Thompson*, the crew of the *Wilfred Sykes* managed to pull deckhand Kenneth L. Kumm from a half-flooded lifeboat before the turbulent waters of the lake tore it

The *Wilfred Sykes* about to enter the Davis Lock at Sault Ste. Marie, Michigan during the summer of 1960.
(Author's Collection)

away from the side of their vessel. To retrieve the wayward craft, the first mate of the Inland steamer, Arthur Ritter, and nine volunteers launched one of their own ship's lifeboats into the cold waters of Lake Superior. This dangerous effort resulted in the rescue of another deckhand named Bernard Oberoski and the recovery of the body of Frank Tomczak, an oiler from Buffalo, New York. In addition to the two survivors pulled aboard the *Wilfred Sykes*, the crew of the *Joseph H. Thompson* rescued five others while that of the *D. M. Clemson* (2) plucked seven more from the lake. Sinking approximately 15 miles south of Isle Royale, the loss of the *Henry*

Steinbrenner (1) cost 17 of its 31 crewmembers their lives.

When the *Wilfred Sykes* arrived at Indiana Harbor on May 14, 1953, Inland Steel recognized the actions of its crew earlier that week by holding an informal shipboard ceremony headed by Philip D. Block Jr., vice president of raw materials, and Wilfred Sykes, the now retired president of the company. Addressing the assembled crew, Block praised their response to the hazards confronted during the rescue operation when he said, "...you not only followed the tradition of the lakes, but you performed heroically in the line of duty." In addition, the company vice president also presented each crewmember with a U.S savings bond in recognition of Inland Steel's appreciation for their actions.

Although surpassed in size and carrying capacity by newer vessels, the *Wilfred Sykes* remained the largest ship in the Inland Steel fleet until the commissioning of the 730-foot long *Edward L. Ryerson* in 1960. In a departure from its regular trading pattern into Indiana Harbor with raw materials, the *Wilfred Sykes* paid a very rare visit to Cleveland, Ohio on September 23, 1968 when it delivered 21,203 gross tons of taconite to the C&P Ore Dock.

Over the years, Inland Steel vessels have come to the rescue of many persons in distress on the heavily traveled Lake Michigan. One such instance occurred on September 25, 1971 when the *Wilfred Sykes* rescued a man in a sailboat off Kenosha, Wisconsin that had been adrift for thirty hours. Although an effort to tow the sailboat failed due to heavy seas, the *Sykes* remained on location until the arrival of the U.S. Coast Guard.

The *Wilfred Sykes* sustained serious bottom damage on August 5, 1973 when it went aground while backing away from the Valley Camp ore dock at Thunder Bay, Ontario. Although able to proceed to Indiana Harbor and then South Chicago under its own power, the steamer required five days worth of repairs in a dry dock before resuming service.

In 1975, Inland Steel had the *Wilfred Sykes* converted into a self-unloader by the Fraser Shipyards at Superior, Wisconsin. This conversion increased the efficiency of this vessel by eliminating its dependence upon shore side unloading equipment while also increasing the number of ports it could serve outside of its long-established trading pattern into Indiana Harbor. Unlike traditional self-unloading conversions of U.S. flagged lake freighters that resulted in forward mounted booms, this reconstruction involved the installation of a stern mounted unloading boom in a manner similar to that pioneered by the *Frontenac* (3) of the Canada Steamship Lines in 1973. The self-unloading system also differed from earlier installations in that it used a loop belt system that sandwiched cargo between two separate conveyor belts to reach the topside boom conveyor in contrast to traditional bucket elevator and inclined conveyor systems. In addition to the *Wilfred Sykes*, the Interlake Steamship Company's *Herbert C. Jackson* received a similar self-unloading configuration during its reconstruction by the Defoe Shipbuilding Company at Bay City, Michigan that same year. Proving popular, all U.S. flagged ships converted to self-unloaders since 1975 have incorporated stern mounted booms. One pending exception to this rule is represented by the planned conversion of the long-idled *John Sherwin* (2), which was to be rebuilt to a bow mounted unloading boom configuration prior to the project being stalled by economic conditions in 2008.

Completed during the first week of July 1975, the *Wilfred Sykes* departed Fraser Shipyards to load 23,905 gross tons of taconite at the nearby Burlington Northern ore docks. Using its 250-foot long unloading boom, this steamer discharged its first cargo as a self-unloader at Indiana Harbor on July 9, 1975. Four months after reentering service, the *Wilfred Sykes* participated in the search for survivors from the *Edmund Fitzgerald* following that steamer's sinking seventeen miles north of Whitefish Point in Lake Superior on November 10, 1975. When this search effort failed to locate any of the *Fitzgerald*'s missing crewmembers, the *Sykes* continued its downbound voyage to Indiana Harbor.

The self-unloading conversion not only minimized the amount of time the *Wilfred Sykes* spent at Inland Steel's unloading dock, it also allowed the steamer to deliver cargoes to outside customers. As such, this ship was to become a common sight at many Lake Michigan ports, including Grand Haven, Holland, Muskegon, and Milwaukee.

The 1980s proved a turning point for the Great Lakes shipping industry. The major recession endured by the domestic steel industry during that decade translated into a dramatic reduction in the demand for the movement of raw materials on the Great Lakes/St. Lawrence Seaway system. This resulted in many ships being laid up for extended periods due to a lack of available cargoes. A good portion of the affected vessels, some less than 30 years old at the time, would never operate again. Although spending some time at the wall during the turbulent times of the early 1980s, Inland Steel managed to find enough work for the *Wilfred Sykes* throughout most of the decade due to the steamer's ability to operate in other trades.

On January 6, 1984, the *Wilfred Sykes* suffered extensive mechanical damage from an explosion in the furnace of its port boiler. Two years later, on September 14, 1986, the *Sykes* paid a rare visit to Detroit, Michigan when it

The steamer *Wilfred Sykes* following its 1975 conversion into a self-unloader. (Author's Collection)

unloaded a cargo of limestone at the Great Lakes Steel dock on Zug Island in the Detroit River. This was apparently the steamer's first voyage to this area since passing through in October 1976 to deliver a cargo of iron ore to Ashtabula.

A combination of high winds and a strong current caused the *Wilfred Sykes* to ram a seawall while inbound at Grand Haven, Michigan on April 2, 1997. Entering that port as the first commercial vessel of the season, the *Sykes* was carrying a cargo of slag destined for delivery to the Verplank Trucking Company dock at Ferrysburg,

Michigan. Although smashing a 60-foot section of the seawall, the *Sykes* sustained no significant damage from this early season incident.

When Ispat International purchased the Inland Steel Company in 1998, ownership of the *Wilfred Sykes* transferred to the Indiana Harbor Steamship Co. to comply with the regulatory requirements of the Jones Act. Concurrent with this transaction, Central Marine Logistics assumed management of this steamer and the two other former Inland Steel vessels, *Joseph L. Block* and *Edward L. Ryerson*. To reflect the change in ownership, all references to Inland Steel, including the large billboard lettering on the hull, soon disappeared from the *Wilfred Sykes* and its fleet mates.

In April of 1998, the *Wilfred Sykes* made a rare trip to the lower lakes after loading a cargo of iron ore at Escanaba for delivery to Ashtabula, Ohio. On August 11 of that same year, this steamer encountered more difficulties at Grand Haven when it grounded on the soft bottom of the Grand River before freeing itself a short time later.

To celebrate the fiftieth anniversary of its launching at Lorain, Ohio and its entry into service the following year, the *Wilfred Sykes* operated throughout the 1999 and 2000 shipping seasons with "50 yrs of Smooth Sailing!" painted in script lettering on its pilothouse.

Shortly after arriving at Muskegon, Michigan on the

evening of November 13, 2002, the *Wilfred Sykes* ran aground in Muskegon Lake. At the time of the stranding, this steamer was inbound with a cargo of limestone. Despite the efforts of the tugs *Mari Beth Andrie* and *Undaunted*, the *Sykes* refused to budge from the bottom throughout the following morning. The stranded steamer finally broke free later that afternoon after unloading a portion of its cargo into the barge *Pere Marquette 41*. Undamaged in the incident, the *Wilfred Sykes* continued to the West Michigan Dock & Market Corporation dock to deliver the balance of its payload.

Since the 1980s, this vessel has concentrated on serving ports on Lake Michigan with an occasional trip to Lake Superior for taconite. As such, common loading ports are Escanaba, Port Inland, and Cedarville.

On April 9, 2002, the *Wilfred Sykes* paid its first visit to the Saginaw River when it discharged a stone cargo loaded at Stoneport, Michigan to the Wirt Stone docks located in Bay City and Saginaw, Michigan. That same season, this versatile ship also became active in carrying iron ore from Marquette to Rouge Steel's Dearborn, Michigan complex on the Rouge River south of Detroit. Representing a major departure from its normal trading routes on Lake Michigan, the *Wilfred Sykes* conducted several such voyages with trips to the Rouge and Saginaw rivers continuing through the 2004 and 2005 shipping seasons respectively.

With its late and early season loadings taking place at Escanaba, the *Wilfred Sykes* is usually one of the last U.S. flagged carriers to layup at the end of the season and one of the earliest to reactivate with the coming of spring. Since first entering service in 1950 as the largest ship on the Great Lakes, this steamer has enjoyed an active and lengthy career. Over the intervening years since sailing on its maiden voyage, the *Wilfred Sykes* has become one of the smaller and among the oldest vessels currently operating within the U.S. fleet.

Chapter Eleven
Steamer *Edward L. Ryerson*

The construction of the St. Lawrence Seaway during the 1950s included improvements to many channels around the Great Lakes that permitted the building of larger vessels. By 1959, the maximum vessel dimensions allowed passage through the locks in this waterway system had increased to a length of 730 feet and 75 feet in beam. These dimensions proved very popular for Canadian ship owners as they rebuilt their fleets during the 1960s to take advantage of the newly opened St. Lawrence Seaway. Meanwhile, construction of U.S. flagged vessels for use on the lakes was nearing a standstill as the 1950s drew to a close. This followed a decade-long period of new ship construction that began with the commissioning of the *Wilfred Sykes* in 1950. As such, the U.S. flagged fleet saw the addition of only two 730-foot vessels built from the keel up before all new construction came to a halt in 1960. These two vessels were Bethlehem Steel's *Arthur B. Homer* and Inland Steel's *Edward L. Ryerson*. With a length just 9 inches shorter than these two vessels, however, the *Edmund Fitzgerald* is arguably a member of this same class. While the *Arthur*

B. Homer followed the same general design pioneered by the *Fitzgerald* in 1958, Inland Steel's new steamer was to be unlike any other to have sailed the Great Lakes before, or since.

Designed by the naval architecture firm H. C. Downer & Associates of Cleveland, Ohio, the Inland Steel Company chose Manitowoc Shipbuilding of Manitowoc, Wisconsin to build their new $8 million steamer. This contract was unique in the fact that with the exception of the motor vessel *The Inland*, every ship operated by the Inland fleet up to this time had come from the yards of the American Ship Building Company or that firm's subsidiary, the West Bay City Shipbuilding Company. Optimized specifically for the transport of iron ore, the cabins of this vessel incorporated a number of modernistic aesthetic features styled by industrial designer Karl Brocken.

On April 20, 1959, shipyard workers laid the keel for the *Edward L. Ryerson* during a modest ceremony held to commemorate the occasion. After receiving a signal from the vessel's namesake, crane operators lowered an 8-ton keel section onto the blocks upon which the massive vessel was to take shape during the upcoming months. The Inland Steel delegation accompanying Edward L. Ryerson to this event included Carl B. Jacobs, company vice president, Riley O'Brien, fleet manager, and Larry J. Sunderlie, assistant fleet manager.

With the transport of iron ore representing a primary design requirement, the *Edward L. Ryerson* featured a cargo hold arrangement possessing significantly lower cubic foot dimensions than those of similar sized carriers. This was due to the simple fact that the specific gravity of iron ore is higher than that of other cargoes such as coal, stone, and grain. As the carriage of ore requires less space to reach a vessel's maximum draft compared other cargoes routinely transported on the lakes, it was therefore unnecessary for Inland's steamer to have a cargo hold with large cubic dimensions. A direct comparison of the *Edward L. Ryerson* and *Arthur B. Homer* reveals the substantial difference in the cubic capacities between these two ships. Although both vessels shared identical overall dimensions, the *Homer's* three cargo holds possessed a cumulative 860,950 cubic feet of space, while the four such compartments in the *Ryerson* totaled only 761,000 cubic feet. With their ore carrying capabilities nearly identical, the *Arthur B. Homer* (at its original 730-foot length) was able to carry 19,170 net tons of coal to the *Ryerson's* capacity of only 14,700 net tons of the same material.

At the time of its construction, the square configuration of the *Edward L. Ryerson's* cargo holds was widely touted as a method of improving unloading times while also decreasing the potential of damage by shore side unloading equipment. Despite these benefits, however, this design feature has complicated this vessel's suitability to receive a self-unloading conversion similar to that given to the *Wilfred Sykes* and several other vessels built during the same timeframe.

Braving 10-degree temperatures, a crowd estimated at 5,000 gathered around the Manitowoc Shipbuilding yard on the morning of January 21, 1960 in anticipation of viewing the *Edward L. Ryerson* launch into an ice-filled Manitowoc River. Missing on her first try, Mrs. Edward L. Ryerson christened her husband's namesake just before noon that morning when she smashed a bottle of champagne against the prow of the massive hull. Moments later, the vessel slid sideways into the river as those in the crowd cheered from their vantage points on shore. The *Edward L. Ryerson* first entered its element at 11:58 a.m. that winter morning, two minutes ahead of its scheduled noon launch.

With a length of 730 feet, a beam of 75 feet, and a 39 foot depth, the *Edward L. Ryerson* was able to carry 27,000 gross tons of iron ore, although subsequent load line revisions resulted in this steamer's carrying capacity increasing to 27,500 gross tons. Powered by a 9,900 shaft horsepower General Electric steam turbine, this vessel has a service speed of 14.5 knots (16.75 mph). Equipped with two Combustion Engineering oil-fired water tube boilers, the *Ryerson* has the capacity to carry 214,900 gallons of fuel oil.

To complement its stylized cabins, the design of the *Edward L. Ryerson* also included a large streamlined stack fabricated from stainless steel. Installed aboard the steamer on May 23, 1960, the stack housed air conditioning and ventilation machinery in addition to the exhaust piping from the engine room. Retaining stainless steel as its base color, the stack markings of the *Ryerson* differed from the rest of the Inland Steel fleet by only incorporating a wide red stripe at its top and a red diamond logo with the word "INLAND" in white lettering. A subsequent revision to the Inland diamond logo during the late 1970s resulted in the replacement of the word "INLAND" with a large "I" in block case lettering.

In preparation for its sea trials, the *Edward L. Ryerson* was moved from the shipyard to the Rahr dock located on Manitowoc's lakefront. This required four tugs to guide the 730-foot freighter through the confines of the Manitowoc River during a 4 ½ hour journey on July 28, 1960. The most delicate part of this operation involved passage through the Soo Line railroad bridge. In addition to the bridge opening being less than 20 feet wider than the beam of the *Ryerson*, the tugs had to take the steamer through a 90-degree turn after passing through the bridge. As the length of the newly built steamer prevented it from clearing the bridge before beginning the turn, workers had previously excavated a 30-foot section of shoreline approximately 300 feet long to provide the extra room necessary for this maneuver. With the *Ryerson*'s bow pushed into the notched out section of shoreline, tugs gently moved the stern past the bridge opening. This major obstacle behind them, the tugs backed the bulk carrier away from the shore and

Tugs maneuver the *Edward L. Ryerson* on the Manitowoc River on July 28, 1960. Excavation work done to the riverbank to allow the 730-foot long steamer make its passage from the shipyard to Lake Michigan is evident at the vessel's bow. (Author's Collection)

proceeded towards Lake Michigan. With the trend towards larger ships proving an insurmountable obstacle to Manitowoc Shipbuilding's facility at Manitowoc, the *Edward L. Ryerson* was the last ship built at that city.

Following its successful sea trials on August 1, 1960, the *Edward L. Ryerson* departed Manitowoc three days later bound for Escanaba, Michigan. Loading 23,378 gross tons of iron ore for delivery to Indiana Harbor, Indiana on August 5, this ship established a new Great Lakes cargo record on its maiden voyage. Although this bested the 23,051 gross ton record set by the *Edmund Fitzgerald* at Silver Bay, Minnesota on July 8 of that year, it soon fell to the *Arthur B. Homer*'s 23,922 gross ton cargo loaded at Taconite Harbor, Minnesota on August 22, 1960.

The *Edward L. Ryerson* was destined to remain one of the largest ships on the Great Lakes until the commissioning of the *Stewart J. Cort* in 1972. On August 28, 1962, this steamer established a new Great Lakes cargo record when it loaded 25,018 gross tons of iron ore at the Great Northern Railway's dock at Superior, Wisconsin for delivery to Indiana Harbor. This record stood until broken by a Canadian flagged carrier in 1965.

Inland Steel had a long tradition of providing trips to guests aboard their vessels, among which included members of the steelmaker's management and representatives from important customers. As such, the

The *Edward L. Ryerson* making its maiden voyage into Indiana Harbor, Indiana. (Author's Collection)

forward section of the *Edward L. Ryerson* included four double berth staterooms and a nicely outfitted owner's lounge overlooking the spar deck facing aft. Serving as a centerpiece in the latter compartment, was a large stainless steel map of the Great Lakes. On this display, the crew moved a small magnetic representation of the *Ryerson* to its appropriate position to keep the guests informed of the ship's current location.

During the 1960s, the use of bow thrusters became common on the Great Lakes with several existing ships receiving such modifications. Consisting of a tunnel with

137

a propeller unit inside, this device acts much like a tugboat by pushing the bow of a vessel in the desired direction from a control panel in the pilothouse. Such installations greatly improved docking operations and lowered the workload of lock passages while also reducing reliance on tugs. Realizing the benefits of these units, Inland Steel had a bow thruster installed in the *Edward L. Ryerson* in 1965.

Throughout the 1960s and 1970s, the *Edward L. Ryerson* remained busy transporting iron ore into Inland's mill at Indiana Harbor. During this time, this ship remained a gearless bulk carrier despite the conversion of the *Wilfred Sykes* into a self-unloader in 1975. The following year, the newly commissioned *Joseph L. Block,* with its 37,200 gross ton carrying capacity, replaced the *Ryerson* as the Inland fleet's largest ship. These factors along with a major recession in the domestic steel industry during the early 1980s resulted in the *Edward L. Ryerson* entering into a cycle of extended periods of idleness that continue to this day.

Since entering service in 1960, the *Edward L. Ryerson* has not been involved in any incident of serious consequence. Committed to the delivery of iron ore into Indiana Harbor, this unique ship has spent most of its operational career in a trading pattern extending from that port to Escanaba and loading ports on Lake Superior. By the mid

-1980s, the *Ryerson* had become the last gearless bulk carrier operating exclusively in the ore trade under the U.S. flag.

On August 21, 1989, the *Edward L. Ryerson* paid its first visit to Detroit, Michigan when it made a rare trip to load mill scale at the Great Lakes Steel dock on Zug Island for delivery to Indiana Harbor. Clearing five days later following some loading delays, this steamer made an identical voyage in November of that year. Although the appearance of the *Edward L. Ryerson* in this region of the

The *Edward L. Ryerson* downbound at Mission Point on the St. Marys River during the late 1960s. (M. J. Brown photo)

Great Lakes was extremely rare at the time, subsequent events some twenty years later would result in this steamer operating regularly in these waters. This ship's departure from its regular trade routes continued during the 1990 and 1991 shipping seasons with trips to Rogers City, Michigan to load stone for Indiana Harbor.

Following three years of inactivity, the *Edward L. Ryerson* returned to service on April 5, 1997 when it departed Sturgeon Bay, Wisconsin to load its first cargo of the season at Escanaba. Two days later, this steamer suffered a loss of power due to boiler problems while downbound

The *Edward L. Ryerson*'s unique stainless steel stack is evident in this early view of the steamer upbound on the St. Marys River. (M. J. Brown photo)

on Lake Michigan north of Milwaukee, Wisconsin. Towed into Milwaukee harbor on the morning of April 8 by the tug *Superior*, the *Ryerson* departed for Indiana Harbor the following day after receiving repairs.

As with the other ships owned by Inland Steel, the steelmaker's 1998 acquisition by Ispat International resulted in the *Ryerson*'s ownership transferring to the Indiana Harbor Steamship Company. This transaction also resulted in the establishment of Central Marine Logistics, Inc. to manage the operation of the *Edward L. Ryerson*, and its two fleet mates, the *Joseph L. Block* and *Wilfred Sykes*. Although retaining its basic color scheme, the "INLAND STEEL" billboard lettering soon disappeared from the steamer's hull to reflect the change in ownership. Entering into an extended period of layup shortly afterwards, the *Ryerson*'s stack markings remained untouched at this time.

While in extended layup at Sturgeon Bay, the *Edward L. Ryerson* was opened for public tours during the summer of 2002 and the spring of 2003 to raise funds for that city's Door County Maritime Museum. The first of these open houses took place during the weekend of July 20-21, 2002, proved extremely popular with over 1,200 people taking the rare opportunity to tour the classic steamer during that two-day period.

Returning to service in July 2006 after nearly eight years

of idleness, the *Edward L. Ryerson* soon entered into a regular pattern of carrying taconite between the Burlington Northern ore dock at Superior, Wisconsin and the Jonick dock at Lorain, Ohio in addition to occasional deliveries to Indiana Harbor. With no permanent shore side equipment at Lorain, unloading of the bulk carrier at that port involved the use of three cranes equipped with clamshell buckets. Following the *Ryerson*'s first arrival at this location on August 20, 2006, the hourly unloading rates provided by the cranes improved significantly during subsequent deliveries as their crews became more familiar with the operation.

As can be expected for a vessel resuming operation following a prolonged period of inactivity, the *Edward L. Ryerson* encountered a series of minor mechanical problems that prompted stops at the Fraser Shipyards, Bay Shipbuilding, and the Carbide dock at Sault Ste. Marie, Michigan. Prior to entering service, the *Ryerson* received new stack markings in the form of a blue band on its top and the word "MITTAL" in black lettering. Operating late into the winter months, this steamer closed the Soo Locks for the 2006 navigation season when it locked downbound with taconite at 2 a.m. on January 16, 2007.

In addition to continuing its deliveries to Indiana Harbor and Lorain during the 2007 shipping season, the *Edward*

The *Edward L. Ryerson* downbound in the MacArthur Lock during the 1997 shipping season. (R. Strauss photo)

L. Ryerson also transited the Welland Canal and the St. Lawrence Seaway for the first time in its career when it began carrying ore to Quebec City, Quebec. During the 2007-2008 winter layup, the *Ryerson* had its stack markings replaced with a black band at its top, the words "ArcelorMittal" in black lettering, and the steelmaker's logo. Resuming its trips to Lorain and Indiana Harbor in 2008, the *Ryerson* also began making ore deliveries to ArcelorMittal's Dofasco steel mill at Hamilton, Ontario. Making a handful of trips to Hamilton with ore at the very beginning of the 2009 shipping season, the *Edward L. Ryerson* remained in service until a lingering economic downturn that began late the previous year forced Central Marine Logistics to place this ship into layup in mid-May of that year.

As stated earlier, a cycle of idleness has characterized this steamer's career since the early 1980s. Following the 1985 shipping season, the *Edward L. Ryerson* has been laid up for extended periods on four separate occasions. Laying up at Indiana Harbor on December 11 of that year, economic conditions kept this steamer idled until it returned to service in the ore trade on March 26, 1988. Remaining active until January 24, 1994, the *Edward L. Ryerson* entered layup on that date at the Bay Shipbuilding yard at Sturgeon Bay, Wisconsin. Inland Steel's charter of the *Adam E. Cornelius* (4) beginning with the 1994 shipping season relegated the *Ryerson* to a backup status. As such, this straight deck bulk carrier remained at Sturgeon Bay until the demand for ore movement improved sufficiently to warrant its return to active service on April 5, 1997. Operating throughout that season and the next primarily carrying ore from Marquette, Michigan to Indiana Harbor, the *Edward L. Ryerson* laid up at Sturgeon Bay on December 12, 1998. After spending nearly eight years in layup, another increase in demand for ore movement on the Great Lakes led to the reactivation of the long-idled steamer. Departing Bay Shipbuilding on July 22, 2006, the *Edward L. Ryerson* operated in the ore trade until reentering a long-term layup status at the Fraser Shipyards at Superior, Wisconsin on May 18, 2009. As of the 2015 shipping season, this ship has not yet reentered active service.

Chapter Twelve
Steamer *J. J. Sullivan*

The steamer *J. J. Sullivan* came into the Inland Steel fleet on May 17, 1962 following its purchase from the Pioneer Steamship Company for $325,000. This transaction came at a time in which that fleet was undergoing a process of vessel liquidation while entering its final days of operation. In fact, the sale of the *Sullivan* came just one month before Pioneer's shareholders voted to dissolve the company, thus bringing about the end of a shipping fleet dating back to 1901.

Launched on September 14, 1907 at Cleveland, Ohio by the American Ship Building Company, the *J. J. Sullivan* entered service for the Superior Steamship Company in October of that same year. Established specifically to operate the *Sullivan*, the Superior Steamship Company was one of several smaller companies established by the Hutchinson fleet to limit its overall liability. Measuring 552 feet in length, this ship had a 56-foot beam and a 31-foot depth and was one of a large number of vessels built to those dimensions during the early twentieth century. In its original form, the *J. J. Sullivan*'s power plant consisted of a 1,765 indicated horsepower triple-expansion steam engine and two Scotch boilers. Fabrication of both the engines and boilers took place at the constructing shipyard.

The *J. J. Sullivan* operated for the Superior Steamship Company until 1913, when Hutchinson merged this company, along with the Ohio and Tonopah Steamship companies, into its larger Pioneer Steamship Company.

During 1918, this ship was involved in two separate

The *Clarence B. Randall* (2) passing the Edison Sault Hydroelectric Plant at Sault Ste. Marie, Michigan in preparation to enter the Soo Locks. (Author's Collection)

incidents. The first occurred during the early navigation season when on April 28 the *J. J. Sullivan* hit bottom in the upper St. Marys River while downbound with iron ore for delivery to Indiana Harbor. Caused when the captain of the *Sullivan* maneuvered his ship too close to the edge of the channel to avoid striking another vessel, the bottom damage from this incident resulted in an $11,400 repair bill. Just eight days later, on May 6, 1918, the *J. J. Sullivan* suffered ice damage while carrying iron ore from Two Harbors, Minnesota to Cleveland, Ohio. In addition to the *Sullivan*, the heavy ice conditions existing in eastern Lake Superior during early May of that year also inflicted damage to four other freighters. Repairs to the Pioneer steamer from this instance amounted to just under $10,000.

The *J. J. Sullivan*'s string of early season difficulties continued into the following year, when it was involved in a potentially more catastrophic incident. This took place on April 16, 1919 when the steamer grounded on De Tour Reef while upbound in a spring snowstorm. Owing to the earliness of the navigational season, a significant contributing factor in this accident was the absence of the buoy normally marking this underwater hazard. Luckily, the grounding did not prove serious with the *Sullivan* managing to extricate itself from the reef once the weather cleared with relatively minor hull damage, which required subsequent repairs at Superior, Wisconsin.

In 1950, Pioneer had the *Sullivan* repowered with a 2,400 indicated horsepower Skinner Unaflow steam engine built by the Skinner Engine Company of Erie, Pennsylvania. This process also included the replacement of the vessel's original Scotch boilers with two Foster-Wheeler water tube boilers. In contrast to some repowering projects undertaken on the Great Lakes during this period that involved conversion to oil as fuel, the *J. J. Sullivan* remained coal-fired.

On November 15, 1956, the *J. J. Sullivan* encountered a heavy fall storm while upbound in Lake Michigan. Struggling throughout the balance of that day and all through the next, the battered steamer finally reached the safety of the St. Marys River on the morning of November 17 but not before suffering some $20,000 worth of structural damage.

A further incident occurred during the following season, when the *J. J. Sullivan* ran aground in the Amherstburg Channel south of Detroit on October 30, 1957. At the time of the grounding, this steamer was carrying a cargo of coal loaded at Sandusky, Ohio for delivery to Indiana Harbor. Released later that day by the tug *Maine*, the *Sullivan* resumed its trip after an inspection revealed no serious damage. Subsequent repairs took place at the

Great Lakes Engineering Works at River Rouge, Michigan over a three-day period beginning on November 12, 1957.

While carrying a cargo of iron ore from Superior to Indiana Harbor on July 22, 1958, the *J. J. Sullivan* struck an underwater obstruction near De Tour, Michigan as it left the St. Marys River to enter Lake Huron. Discovering water leaking into the No. 3 starboard ballast tank, the steamer's crew reversed course and anchored in the lower St. Marys River. After a further survey of the hull leakage, the authorities permitted the *J. J. Sullivan* to deliver its cargo to Inland Steel before returning to Superior for repairs. Entering the dry dock on July 28, the *Sullivan* required $75,000 worth of repairs that took shipyard workers eight days to complete.

Following this incident, the *J. J. Sullivan* served its last remaining years in the Pioneer fleet without encountering any further mishaps of note prior to its before mentioned sale to Inland Steel in 1962. Repainted in Inland Steel fleet colors, this ship entered service for its new owner under its original name before being renamed *Clarence B. Randall* (2) later that year.

With the grounding and subsequent sale of the *Joseph Block* in 1968, the *Clarence B. Randall* (2) became the last steamship ever operated by Inland Steel powered by a reciprocating engine. One of the primary duties fulfilled by this vessel in the Inland fleet was the movement of raw materials between the steelmaker's plants at Indiana Harbor. Navigation between these facilities was complicated by a series of railroad bridges crossing the Indiana Harbor Ship Canal that had draw spans only 65 feet wide. As was the case with the identically sized *E. J. Block*, the 56-foot beam of the *Clarence B. Randall* (2) permitted passage through these narrow openings.

When not required in the transshipment role, this steamer made trips up Lake Michigan to load ore at Escanaba or even more uncommon voyages to Lake Superior. On one such trip to the northernmost of the five

The *Clarence B. Randall* (2) downbound in the St. Marys River near the end of its operational career. (James Hoffman photo)

Great Lakes, the *Clarence B. Randall* (2) participated in the first double vessel transit through the newly built Poe Lock at Sault Ste. Marie, Michigan when it locked through with Paterson's 291-foot *Mondoc* (3) on October 28, 1969.

While having a relatively quiet career following its acquisition by Inland Steel, the *Clarence B. Randall* (2) did suffer at least one accident near the end of its operational career. This occurred on August 8, 1973 when this steamer ran aground in Lake Munuscong while transiting the St. Marys River in a dense fog. The grounding proved minor in nature, however, as the *Randall* (2) managed to free itself from the bottom about an hour later without sustaining any damage.

The *Clarence B. Randall* (2) remained active in the Inland Steel fleet until being laid up for the final time in September of 1976. Sold to the Afram Brothers Company of Milwaukee, Wisconsin for non-transportation use in November of that same year, the *Randall* (2) was to spend ten years of idleness at that port. While undergoing a conversion to a floating dock, a fire erupted aboard the retired steamer on March 14, 1980. Ignited by a cutting torch, this blaze damaged the vessel's galley and three staterooms.

Subsequently sold to the North Central Maritime Corporation of Duluth, Minnesota for use as a grain storage barge, the *Clarence B. Randall* (2) was to be renamed *Wannamingo*, but was never officially registered under that name. After purchasing the *Randall* (2) for scrap in early 1987, Corostel Trading Ltd. of Montreal, Quebec resold the retired vessel to M&M Steel of Windsor, Ontario. In an unusual wintertime scrap tow, the tugs *Glenada* and *Tusker* pulled the *Clarence B. Randall* (2) out of Milwaukee on January 16, 1987. Leaving the Wisconsin port behind, the trio arrived at Windsor three days later, where scrapping of the former Inland Steel steamer took place later that year.

Chapter Thirteen
Motor Vessel *Joseph L. Block*

Launched by the Bay Shipbuilding Corporation at Sturgeon Bay, Wisconsin on February 26, 1976, the *Joseph L. Block* was the largest vessel ever constructed for the Inland Steel Company. Although the *Wilfred Sykes* had undergone a conversion into a self-unloader one year earlier, the *Block* was also the first ship built for the Inland fleet capable of unloading without the use of shore side equipment. In addition, the *Joseph L. Block* was the first diesel-powered freighter constructed for the steelmaker. Despite this, the fleet had gained previous experience operating such vessels following the postwar conversion of the *E. J. Block* and its ownership of the motor vessel *The Inland* during a brief two-year period stretching from 1946 -1948. When Mrs. Joseph L. Block smashed a bottle of champagne against her husband's namesake on June 29, 1976, none of those gathered to witness the christening ceremony could have known that the massive vessel before them was to be the last ship ever built for the Inland Steel fleet.

Its construction and sea trials complete, the *Joseph L. Block* began its maiden voyage on August 15, 1976 when it departed Sturgeon Bay bound for Escanaba, Michigan, where it loaded 32,607 gross tons of taconite pellets for delivery to Indiana Harbor. At 728 feet in length, 78 feet in beam, and 45 feet in depth, this vessel can carry a maximum of 37,200 gross tons of iron ore pellets at a draft of 30 feet 11 inches. Fitted with a 250-foot long conveyor boom, the *Joseph L. Block* can unload its cargoes at a rate of 6,000 tons per hour. Mounted directly in front of the superstructure at a point 110 feet from the stern, the boom can pivot up to 105 degrees in either direction of the vessel's centerline. Powered by a pair of 3,500 brake horsepower diesel engines built by General Motors' Electro-Motive Division (EMD), the *Block* has a rated speed of 15 knots. To assist this vessel's operation in constrained quarters, it is equipped with both bow and stern thrusters.

Built specifically to haul raw materials into Inland Steel's manufacturing complex at Indiana Harbor, the *Joseph L. Block* entered operation primarily on trade routes extending from that port to Escanaba and loading points in western Lake Superior. Early in its career, however, this ship made a rare trip to Lake Erie when it delivered 30,306 tons of taconite to the Pinney Dock at Ashtabula, Ohio on October 12, 1976. The *Block* was one three vessels that together unloaded a record 108,379 tons of ore at the Pinney Dock on that date. The other vessels involved in

Pushing its way down the St. Marys River in July of 1987, the *Joseph L. Block* heads to Indiana Harbor with another cargo of taconite pellets. (Tom Salvner photo)

this record setting achievement were the *Wilfred Sykes*, on an equally rare trip to Lake Erie, and the Interlake Steamship Company's recently commissioned *James R. Barker*.

Throughout this vessel's career, Escanaba has remained a popular loading port. This is particularly true when the winter season forces the closure of the locks at Sault Ste. Marie, thereby precluding any commerce between Lake Superior and the lower lakes. As such, the *Joseph L. Block* and its fleet mate *Wilfred Sykes* are usually the first vessels to enter service each spring while also being among the last to enter winter layup. During one of its many late season trips, the *Joseph L. Block* ran into trouble when it went aground at Escanaba on January 6, 1990. Proceeding to Indiana Harbor following the incident to unload its cargo of taconite, the *Block* returned up Lake Michigan to enter layup at the Bay Shipbuilding yard at Sturgeon Bay. The severity of this incident proved much greater than initially thought when a dry-docking in March of that year revealed this ship had suffered an estimated $2.5 million in bottom damages. Following a month long period of extensive repair work, the *Joseph L. Block* returned to service on April 24, 1990 when it departed the shipyard to load ore at Escanaba.

Less than six months later, on October 12, 1990, the *Joseph L. Block* experienced trouble once again when it ran aground in the lower St. Marys River while upbound in a dense fog. Managing to free itself without outside assistance, the *Block* tied up at the Carbide Dock at Sault Ste. Marie, Michigan for a U.S. Coast Guard inspection before proceeding to the Fraser Shipyards at Superior, Wisconsin for repairs.

Shortly after leaving Escanaba with a load of iron ore on March 18, 1997, the *Joseph L. Block* suffered ice damage near the Rock Island Passage connecting Green Bay and Lake Michigan. The following day, the *Block* offloaded

3,500 tons of taconite into its chartered fleet mate *Adam E. Cornelius* (4) before continuing its trip to Indiana Harbor.

The 1998 season would see the *Joseph L. Block* trading in some unfamiliar waters as it made a handful of trips to Lake Erie. The first of these came in April of that year when it carried an ore cargo into Ashtabula. Following this initial foray away from its usual trading pattern of delivering cargoes to ports on Lake Michigan, the *Block* conducted further trips to Lake Erie in August and November, among which included one trip into Toledo, Ohio with ore.

Following Ispat International's purchase of Inland Steel in 1998, ownership of the *Joseph L. Block* passed to the Indiana Harbor Steamship Co. while the newly established Central Marine Logistics took over management of the three former Inland Steel fleet vessels. Shortly afterwards, the *Joseph L. Block* had its "INLAND STEEL" billboard lettering painted over and Inland Steel logos removed from its stack to reflect the change in ownership. Remaining committed to the transport of raw materials into Indiana Harbor following this transition, the trade routes served by the *Block* remained untouched by the demise of its former fleet.

Since coming under the management of Central Marine Logistics, the *Joseph L. Block* has been involved in a few minor incidents. While downbound on the St. Marys

River on May 12, 1999, this ship rubbed the bottom as it approached the entrance to the Rock Cut. Nearly eleven years later, on April 18, 2010, the *Joseph L. Block* struck bottom near the De Tour Reef Light while upbound with a cargo of stone. Neither of these incidents resulted in reports of the 728-foot vessel sustaining any significant hull damage.

Over the years, lake freighters have aided a countless number of individuals that found themselves in trouble far away from shore. One such example occurred on September 8, 2006, when the crew of the *Joseph L. Block* rescued a kayaker in the middle of Lake Michigan, some 32 miles off Milwaukee, Wisconsin.

In 2005, Ispat Inland was part of a major consolidation of domestic steel companies that resulted in the formation of Mittal Steel USA. Just two years later, the Mittal Steel Company merged with its former rival Areclor to create ArcelorMittal, which became the world's largest steel company. Throughout these transitions, the *Joseph L. Block* continued operating for Central Marine Logistics on its long established trade routes with the only outward change being the incorporation of new stack markings as the mergers took place.

In December of 2014, the *Joseph L. Block* paid a rare visit to Cleveland, Ohio with a load of ore it had loaded at Silver Bay, Minnesota. After unloading, this ship sailed to

Toledo, where it took on a cargo of coal destined for delivery to Indiana Harbor.

As of 2015, the *Joseph L. Block* remains active in the ore, coal, and stone trades. While much of the taconite carried aboard this ship during the shipping season is loaded at Escanaba, trips to Lake Superior ports remain commonplace. Although its primary duties still revolve around the delivery of raw materials to ArcelorMittal's steel making facility at Indiana Harbor, this ship is also active in transporting cargoes to other destinations. As such, the *Block* has loaded coal at the KCBX Terminal in Chicago, Illinois on several occasions for delivery to various Lake Michigan ports. This vessel is also a familiar sight at the stone loading ports of Port Inland and Cedarville on the southern shore of Michigan's Upper Peninsula.

Chapter Fourteen
Motor Vessel *Adam E. Cornelius (4)*

In 1994, the Inland Steel Company chartered the *Adam E. Cornelius* (4) from the American Steamship Company. Initially reported as being just two years in duration, this arrangement was to continue for five seasons. The arrival of the *Adam E. Cornelius* (4) into the Inland Steel fleet kept the gearless *Edward L. Ryerson* at the wall following its winter lay-up on January 24, 1994 until it reentered service at the beginning of the 1997 shipping season in response to an increased demand in the ore trade.

Built in 1973 by the American Ship Building Company at Toledo, Ohio as the *Roger M. Kyes*, this ship was the first unit to enter service for the American Steamship Company as part of a major fleet modernization program that lasted until the early 1980s. When completed, this process had resulted in the construction of no less than ten new vessels, including two in the thousand-foot class. Launched on March 31, 1973, the *Roger M. Kyes* entered service on August 22 of that year when it departed Toledo bound to load iron ore at Escanaba, Michigan.

Although considerably smaller than the thirteen thousand-footers built during the same period, the 680-

The *Adam E. Cornelius* (4) passing Mission Point on the St. Marys River while upbound with a cargo of stone during the 1996 shipping season. (Author's Collection)

foot long *Rogers M. Kyes* was nonetheless capable of carrying a respectable 28,200 gross tons of iron ore. Built at a cost of $14 million, this ship's design incorporated a self-unloading system capable of discharging its ore cargoes at a rate of 6,000 tons per hour via a 260-foot unloading boom. A 1,000 horsepower bow thruster unit allowed the *Kyes* to serve many of American Steamship's customers located on constricted waterways without relying on tugboat assistance.

During its career, this ship has been involved in a

number of incidents. The first of these took place on September 22, 1976, when the *Roger M. Kyes* ran aground at Buffalo, New York. Holed in two bottom tanks and sustaining other hull damage in the incident, the *Kyes* proceeded to Chicago, Illinois for dry docking and repairs. Two years later, on September 7, 1978, this ship required an assist by the Great Lakes Towing tugs *Maine* and *Maryland* to reach the Great Lakes Steel dock on the Detroit River after losing power on Lake St. Clair.

After discharging its cargo at McLouth Steel at Trenton, Michigan on April 30, 1979, the *Roger M. Kyes* ran aground in the Trenton Channel of the Detroit River. Freed a short time later with the assistance of a local tugboat, the six-year old vessel was able to resume its trip to Toledo.

On July 24, 1983, the *Roger M. Kyes* was involved in a strange incident when its aft mast struck the I-75 freeway bridge crossing over the Rouge River while inbound with a cargo of limestone destined for the Detroit Lime Company. Taking place at 2 o'clock in the morning, the impact bent this ship's mast and destroyed its radar antenna. Its cargo discharged, the Gaelic tugs *Shannon* and *Wicklow* attempted to assist the *Kyes* out of the river at 6 o'clock that evening only to return the self-unloader back to the dock after discovering the damaged mast would not clear the bottom of the bridge. The following day, a work crew from the Nicholson Terminal & Dock Company arrived at the Detroit Lime dock to remove the mast. Finally able to pass safely beneath the bridge, the *Roger M. Kyes* departed the Rouge River bound for Toledo a short time later.

This vessel's troubles with the Trenton Channel of the Detroit River continued on August 23, 1984 when it went hard aground while en route to the McLouth Steel plant. Proving much more serious than its previous grounding in this same area just five years earlier, the *Roger M. Kyes* came to rest lodged sideways in the narrow channel. When initial refloating efforts failed to free the stranded vessel from the bottom, the *Kyes* used its unloading gear to offload a portion of its cargo into the *Richard J. Reiss* (2). Remaining stubbornly aground for three days, the *Roger M. Kyes* finally floated free on August 26 with the assistance of no less than ten tugs. After unloading the balance of its cargo, this vessel went to the Bay Shipbuilding yard at Sturgeon Bay, Wisconsin for repairs before returning to service on September 26, 1984.

On October 29, 1987, the *Roger M. Kyes* suffered its second serious accident in three years when it ran aground in Lake Erie's Middle Passage while upbound with a cargo of coal loaded at Sandusky, Ohio. Although taking on some water, the *Kyes* managed to free itself the following morning after lightering approximately 3,000 tons of coal into the *American Republic*. This incident required a trip to Bay Shipbuilding, where it entered the dry dock on November 3, 1987 to receive major repairs.

On June 15, 1989 the *Roger M. Kyes* was renamed *Adam E. Cornelius* (4) during a rechristening ceremony at Buffalo, New York. This renaming continued a tradition of the American Steamship Company having a vessel named for Adam E. Cornelius, one its two founding partners, that dated back to 1908. The previous vessel to carry this name had left the American Steamship fleet one year earlier following its sale for conversion into a barge under the Canadian flag as the *Capt. Edward V. Smith*. That vessel was later to become the *Sea Barge One* in 1991 before receiving its current name, *Sarah Spencer*, in 1996.

The *Adam E. Cornelius* (4) operated for the American Steamship Company without incident until its charter to Inland Steel in 1994. Prior to entering service that season, this vessel received Inland Steel colors at Toledo. Although virtually identical to that adorning other members of the steelmaker's fleet, the scheme applied to the *Cornelius* (4) differed by not incorporating the "INLAND STEEL" billboard lettering. Prepared for its new role in supplying Inland Steel's raw material transportation needs, the *Adam E. Cornelius* (4) departed Toledo, without cargo, on May 5, 1994.

A little more than two months into its charter to Inland

The *Adam E. Cornelius* (4) transiting the Saginaw River during the 1999 shipping season following its return to the American Steamship Company. (Author's Collection)

Steel, bad luck struck this ship again when it grounded just north of the upper MacArthur-Poe Lock approach pier at Sault Ste. Marie, Michigan on July 14, 1994. Loaded to a depth of just over 27 feet with a cargo of taconite pellets and veering out of the normal approach lane, the *Adam E. Cornelius* (4) came to a halt partially inside the channel leading to the Davis Lock, which had a depth of only 24 feet. After lightering a portion of its cargo into Interlake's *Elton Hoyt 2nd* (2) the following day, the Great Lakes Towing Company's *Missouri* and the

Purvis tug *Avenger IV* pulled the stranded carrier free from the bottom. Having suffered a puncture in a port side ballast tank, the *Adam E. Cornelius* (4) stopped briefly at the Carbide Dock for an inspection before departing for Indiana Harbor. After unloading its remaining cargo, this ship proceeded to Sturgeon Bay for repairs.

As with other vessels in the Inland Steel fleet, the *Adam E. Cornelius* (4) concentrated on the movement of raw materials into Indiana Harbor. Consequently, Escanaba became a popular loading port along with Duluth and, to a lesser extent, Two Harbors on Lake Superior. On many of its upbound trips to the DM&IR ore dock at Duluth, this ship carried stone cargoes for delivery to that port's Hallet Dock Company.

On January 26, 1997, the *Adam E. Cornelius* (4) experienced serious flooding in a forward compartment after suffering ice damage to its bow on Lake Michigan. Having just departed Escanaba with a load of taconite consigned for Indiana Harbor, the damaged vessel diverted to the Bay Shipbuilding yard at Sturgeon Bay for repairs.

Its charter to Inland Steel having ended at the conclusion of the 1998 shipping season, the *Adam E. Cornelius* (4) reentered service in April of 1999 repainted in American Steamship Company colors. Enjoying a relatively quiet career since returning to its original fleet, this ship serves a variety of routes across the Great Lakes region. In addition to carrying coal, iron ore, and stone, this ship has been active in the grain trade in recent years. Unfortunately, economic conditions have forced the *Adam E. Cornelius* (4) to be idled on several occasions since the beginning of the 2000s. After spending the 2010 season in layup, this ship operated for a partial season in 2011 before reentering a period of idleness that lasted until September of 2014. Laying up at Huron, Ohio at the end of that season, the *Adam E. Cornelius* (4) had not yet reentered service during the 2015 season when this book went to press.

Quick Reference Guide

The following is a brief description of each vessel operated by the Inland Steel Company between 1911 and 1998. The list displays the chronological order in which each vessel first entered the fleet.

Joseph Block. Built: West Bay Shipbuilding Company, West Bay City, Michigan – 1907. Dimensions: 569' x 56' x 31'. Capacity (1966): 11,600 gross tons. Years in fleet: 1911-1968. Official Number: 204631. Notes: Built for the Neptune Steamship Company (Hawgood, mgr.) as *Arthur H. Hawgood*. Sold to the Inland Steamship Company (Hutchinson & Company, mgr.) in 1911. Renamed *Joseph Block* in 1912. Transferred to the Inland Steel Company (Hutchinson & Company, mgr.) in 1936. Grounded in Porte des Morts passage on May 22, 1968 and abandoned to underwriters. Repaired and reentered service as *George M. Steinbrenner* (2) in 1969 for Kinsman Lines. Sold for scrap in 1978.

N. F. Leopold. Built: West Bay Shipbuilding Company, West Bay City, Michigan – 1908. Dimensions: 552' x 56' x 31'. Capacity (1985): 11,500 gross tons. Years in fleet: 1911-1987. Official Number: 205250. Notes: Built for Hawgood Transportation Company as *W. R. Woodford*. Sold to the Inland Steamship Company (Hutchinson & Company, mgr.) in 1911. Transferred to the Inland Steel Company (Hutchinson & Company, mgr.) in 1936. Renamed *N. F. Leopold* in 1912 and *E. J. Block* in 1943. Repowered and refurbished in 1946. Sold for scrap in 1987.

L. E. Block. Built: American Ship Building Company, Lorain, Ohio – 1927. Dimensions: 621' x 64' x 33'. Carrying capacity (1985): 15,900 gross tons. Years in fleet: 1927-1986. Official Number: 226374. Notes: Built for the Inland Steamship Company (Hutchinson & Company, mgr.). Transferred to the Inland Steel Company (Hutchinson & Company, mgr.) in 1936. Sold for non-transportation use in 1986. Sold for scrap in 2006.

Philip D. Block. Built: American Ship Building Company, Lorain, Ohio – 1925. Dimensions: 600' x 60' x 32'. Carrying capacity (1985): 15,400 gross tons. Years in fleet: 1936-1985. Official Number: 224508. Notes: Built for Pioneer Steamship Company (Hutchinson & Company, mgr.). Sold to the Inland Steel Company (Hutchinson & Company, mgr.) in 1936. Lengthened to 672' feet at American Ship Building Company, Chicago, Illinois in 1951. Sold for scrap in 1985.

The Inland. Built: Federal Shipbuilding and Dry Dock Company, Kearney, New Jersey – 1926. Dimensions: 258' 3" x 42' 9" x 20'. Carrying capacity (1946): 2,900 gross tons. Years in fleet: 1946-1948. Official Number: 225935. Notes: Built for United States Steel Products Co. as ***Steel Chemist***. Transferred to the American Steel & Wire Company in 1941. Sold to Inland Steel Company (Hutchinson & Company, mgr.) and renamed ***The Inland*** in 1946. Sold to Transit Tankers & Terminals, Ltd. and converted into a tanker at Port Weller Dry Docks, Ltd., St. Catharines, Ontario in 1948. Renamed ***Transinland*** in 1949. Sold to Hall Corporation in 1968 and renamed ***Inland Transport***. Sold for scrap in 1976.

Wilfred Sykes.   Built: American Ship Building Company, Lorain, Ohio – 1949. Dimensions: 678' x 70' x 37'. Carrying capacity (1998): 21,500 gross tons. Years in fleet: 1949-1998. Official Number: 259193. Notes: Converted to a self-unloader at Fraser Shipyards, Superior, Wisconsin in 1975. Sold to the Indiana Harbor Steamship Company in 1998. Operator (2015): Central Marine Logistics, Incorporated.

Edward L. Ryerson.   Built: Manitowoc Shipbuilding, Inc., Manitowoc, Wisconsin – 1960. Dimensions: 730' x 75' x 39'. Carrying capacity (1998): 27,500 gross tons. Years in fleet: 1960-1998.   Official Number: 282106.   Notes: Sold to the Indiana Harbor Steamship Company in 1998. Laid up at Superior, Wisconsin since 2009. Operator (2015): Central Marine Logistics, Incorporated.

J. J. Sullivan.   Built: American Ship Building Company, Cleveland, Ohio – 1907.   Dimensions: 552' x 56' x 31'. Carrying capacity (1966): 11,100 gross tons. Years in fleet: 1962-1976. Official Number: 204624. Notes: Built for the Superior Steamship Company (Hutchinson & Company, mgr.). Transferred to the Pioneer Steamship Company (Hutchinson & Company, mgr.) in 1915. Sold to the Inland Steel Company and renamed ***Clarence B. Randall*** (2) in 1962. Sold for non-transportation use in 1976. Scrapped in 1987.

Joseph L. Block.   Built: Bay Shipbuilding Corporation, Sturgeon Bay, Wisconsin – 1976. Dimensions: 728' x 78' x 45'. Carrying capacity (1998): 37,200 gross tons. Years in fleet: 1976-1998. Official Number: 574870. Notes: Sold to the Indiana Harbor Steamship Company in 1998. Operator (2015):

Central Marine Logistics, Incorporated.

Adam E. Cornelius (4).   Built: American Ship Building Company, Toledo, Ohio – 1973. Dimensions: 680' x 78' x 42'. Carrying capacity (1998): 28,200 gross tons. Years in fleet: 1994-1998 (Chartered). Official Number: 550520. Notes: Built as ***Roger M. Kyes*** for the American Steamship Company. Renamed ***Adam E. Cornelius*** (4) in 1989. Operator (2015): American Steamship Company.

APPENDICES

<u>Selected Vessel Appointments 1920-1998</u>

The following is a small selection of captain and chief engineer assignments for vessels operated by the Inland Steel Company during various years of the fleet's existence. These listings illustrate both the growth of the fleet and the tough times experienced following the early 1980s. The inactive vessels appearing on the rosters beginning during that decade define the challenges fleet managers faced during times of depressed demand.

<u>1920</u>
Inland Steamship Company
(Managed by Hutchinson & Company)
1508 Rockefeller Building
Cleveland, Ohio

Vessel	**Captain**	**Chief Engineer**
Joseph Block	A. A. Clarke	W. B. Rowe
N. F. Leopold	J. Matthews	F. H. Lang

1954
Inland Steel Company
(Managed by Hutchinson & Company)
1508 Rockefeller Building
Cleveland, Ohio

Vessel	**Captain**	**Chief Engineer**
E. J. Block	T. Olson	A. Seelye
Joseph Block	S. Ward	A. Bringleson
L. E. Block	Wm. Walsh	A. Donald
Philip D. Block	F. Tomlin	J. J. Kronberg
Wilfred Sykes	G. Fisher	A. A. Wolf

1959
Inland Steel Company
30 W. Monroe Street
Chicago, Illinois
Fleet Manager: Riley O'Brien

Vessel	**Captain**	**Chief Engineer**
E. J. Block	T. Olson	A. Seelye
Joseph Block	J. Shoesmith	A. Bringleson
L. E. Block	Wm. Walsh	A. Donald
Philip D. Block	S. Ward	J. J. Kronberg
Wilfred Sykes	G. Fisher	E. Kaarlela

1969

Inland Steel Company
30 W. Monroe Street
Chicago, Illinois
Fleet Manager: Riley O'Brien

Vessel	Captain	Chief Engineer
E. J. Block	D. Paquette	E. Smiley
L. E. Block	C. Miller	J. Mee
Philip D. Block	D. Kinnear	H. Brown
Clarence B. Randall (2)	C. Johnson	T. Burdette
Edward L. Ryerson	J. Shoesmith	B. Wentworth
Wilfred Sykes	J. Leeger	A. Nordbeck

1977

Inland Steel Company
30 W. Monroe Street
Chicago, Illinois
Raw Materials Manager: Sid Bouwer
Asst. Manager Fleet Operations: Larry Sundlie
Assistant Manager Fleet Administration: N. Terry Burton

Vessel	Captain	Chief Engineer
E. J. Block	V. Foshion	J. Schneider
L. E. Block	C. Johnson	J. Mee
Joseph L. Block	D. Paquette	E. Smiley
Philip D. Block	E. Schultz	T. Burdette
Edward L. Ryerson	J. Leeger	J. H. Brown
Wilfred Sykes	P. J. MacMahon	J. L. Williams

1986

Inland Steel Company
30 W. Monroe Street
Chicago, Illinois
Vessel Manager: Bradley F. Sokol

Vessel	**Captain**	**Chief Engineer**
*E. J. Block**		
*L. E. Block**		
Joseph L. Block	V. Foshion	J. Schneider
Edward L. Ryerson	R. Black	J. Woods
Wilfred Sykes	R. Lindquist	L. T. Leonard

*=Inactive

1994

Inland Steel Company
3210 Watling Street
East Chicago, Indiana
Fleet Operations Manager: D. Cornillie

Vessel	**Captain**	**Chief Engineer**
Joseph L. Block	V. Foshion	J. Schneider
Adam E. Cornelius (4)	T. Martineau	M. Lester
*Edward L. Ryerson**		
Wilfred Sykes	R. Brezinski	D. Hunt

*=Inactive

1998
Inland Steel Company
3210 Watling Street
East Chicago, Indiana

Vessel	**Captain**	**Chief Engineer**
Joseph L. Block	M. Miller	R. Baxter
Adam E. Cornelius (4)	T. Martineau	B. Friend
Edward L. Ryerson	R. Brezinski	P. Ilacqua
Wilfred Sykes	R. Sheldon	J. Berg

Fleet Chronology

1911

- *W. R. Woodford* purchased from the Hawgood Transportation Company.
- *Arthur H. Hawgood* purchased from Hawgood's Neptune Steamship Company.
- The Inland Steamship Company, a joint venture between Inland Steel and Hutchinson & Company, incorporated at Charleston, West Virginia.

1912

- *W. R. Woodford* renamed *N. F. Leopold*.
- *Arthur H. Hawgood* renamed *Joseph Block*.

1927

- Inland Steel's first new vessel, *L. E. Block*, enters service.

1936

- *Joseph Block*, *L. E. Block*, and *N. F. Leopold* acquired by the Inland Steel Company during an auction of the Inland Steamship Company's vessels.
- Inland Steamship Company liquidated.
- *Philip D. Block* purchased from Hutchinson & Company's Pioneer Steamship Company.

1943

- *N. F. Leopold* renamed *E. J. Block*.

1946

- Canal-sized motor vessel *Steel Chemist* acquired from the American Steel and Wire Company and renamed *The Inland*.
- *E. J. Block* repowered with diesel-electric propulsion during an extensive refit.

1948

- *The Inland* sold to Transit Tankers and Terminals, Ltd. of Montreal.

1949

- *Wilfred Sykes* launched at Lorain, Ohio as first U.S. flagged postwar lake freighter.

1950

- *Wilfred Sykes* enters service as the largest ship on the Great Lakes.

1951

- *Philip D. Block* lengthened to 672' overall.

1953

- *L. E. Block* repowered.
- *Philip D. Block* repowered.

1956

- Inland Steel ends longstanding fleet management agreement with Hutchinson & Company to manage its own vessels beginning in 1957 .

1960

- *Edward L. Ryerson* enters service.

1962

- *J. J. Sullivan* acquired from the Pioneer Steamship Company and renamed *Clarence B. Randall* (2) later that season.

1968

- *Joseph Block* abandoned to the underwriters following a serious grounding in Lake Michigan.

1975

- *Wilfred Sykes* converted into a self-unloader.

1976

- *Joseph L. Block* enters service.
- *Clarence B. Randall* (2) sold for non-transportation use.

1985

- *Philip D. Block* sold for scrap.

1986

- *L. E. Block* sold for non-transportation use.

1987

- *E. J. Block* sold for scrap.

1994

- *Adam E. Cornelius* (4) chartered from the American Steamship Company.

1998

- Ispat International acquires the Inland Steel Company.
- *Joseph L. Bock*, *Edward L. Ryerson*, and *Wilfred Sykes* sold to the Indiana Harbor Steamship Company to comply with federal regulations.
- Central Marine Logistics, Inc. assumes management of the former Inland Steel vessels.
- *Adam E. Cornelius* (4) charter ends at the close of the navigation season.

<u>Inland Steel Fleet Longevity Table</u>

<u>Rank</u>	<u>Vessel</u>	<u>Member of Fleet</u>	<u>Years in Fleet</u>
1	*N. F. Leopold* (*E. J. Block*)	1911-1987	76
2	*L. E. Block*	1927-1986	59
3	*Joseph Block*	1911-1968	57
4	*Philip D. Block*	1936-1985	49
5	*Wilfred Sykes*	1949-1998	49
6	*Edward L. Ryerson*	1960-1998	38
7	*Joseph L. Block*	1976-1998	22
8	*J. J. Sullivan* (*Clarence B. Randall* (2))	1962-1976	14
9	*Adam E. Cornelius* (4)*	1994-1998	4
10	*The Inland*	1946-1948	2

*=Chartered from the American Steamship Company

Steamer *Edward L. Ryerson*
<u>Long Term Layup Periods 1985-2015</u>

<u>Laid Up</u>	<u>Location</u>	Returned <u>to Service</u>
12/11/1985	Indiana Harbor, Indiana	3/26/1988
1/24/1994	Sturgeon Bay, Wisconsin	4/5/1997
12/12/1998	Sturgeon Bay, Wisconsin	7/22/2006
5/18/2009	Superior, Wisconsin	N/A*

*=Has not returned to service as of press time.

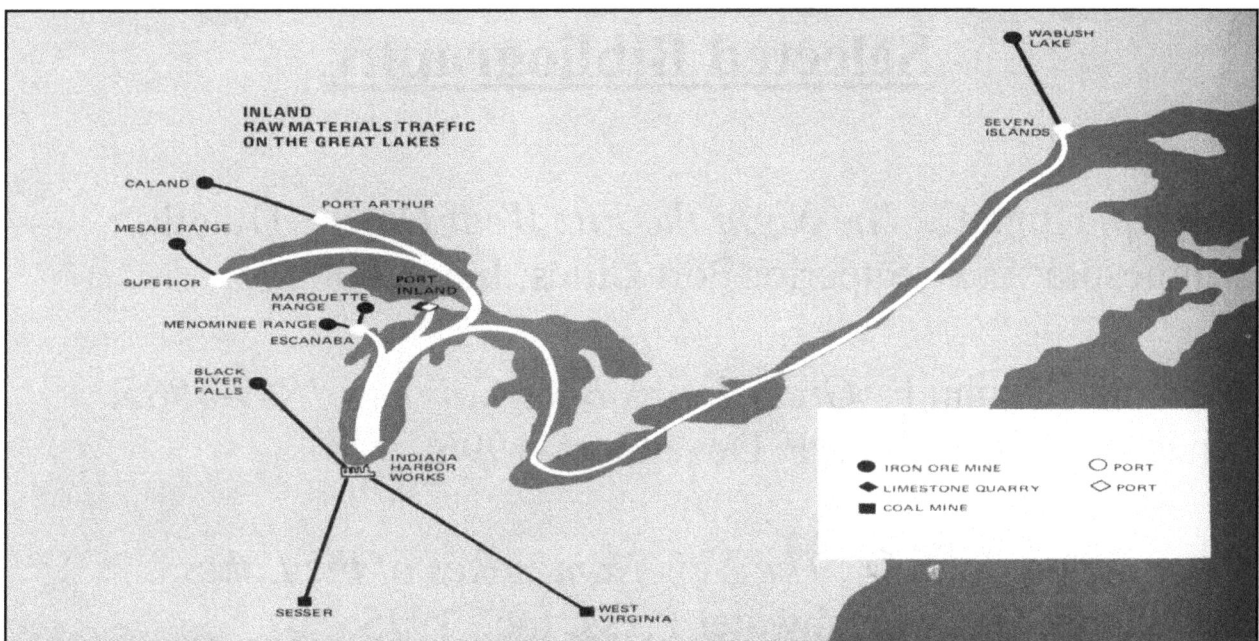

Printed in company brochures by the Inland Steel Company during the early 1970s, this generalized map displays the steelmaker's raw material flow patterns supplying its mill at Indiana Harbor, Indiana. (Author's Collection)

Selected Bibliography

Bishop, Hugh E. *The Night the Fitz Went Down.* Duluth, Minnesota: Lake Superior Port Cities, Inc., 2000.

Devendorf, John F. *Great Lakes Bulk Carriers 1869-1985.* Niles, Michigan: John F. Devendorf, 1996.

Greenwood, John O. *The New Namesakes of the Lakes.* Cleveland, Ohio: Freshwater Press, Inc., 1975.

————. *Namesakes of the 80s.* Cleveland, Ohio: Freshwater Press, Inc., 1980.

————. *Namesakes 1956-1980.* Cleveland, Ohio: Freshwater Press, Inc., 1981.

————. *The Fleet Histories Series, Volume Five.* Cleveland, Ohio: Freshwater Press, Inc., 1998.

————. *The Fleet Histories Series, Volume Six.* Cleveland, Ohio: Freshwater Press, Inc., 1998.

————. *Namesakes 2000.* Cleveland, Ohio: Freshwater Press, Inc., 2000.

Joachim, George J. *Iron Fleet.* Detroit, Michigan: Wayne State University Press, 1994.

The Marine Historical Society of Detroit. *Great Lakes Ships We Remember II.* Cleveland, Ohio: Freshwater Press, 1984.

————. *Great Lakes Ships We Remember III.* Cleveland, Ohio: Freshwater Press 1994.

————. *Ahoy & Farewell II.* Detroit, Michigan: The Marine Historical Society of Detroit, 1996.

————. *Ahoy & Farewell Revised Edition.* Detroit, Michigan: The Marine Historical Society of Detroit, 2001.

Thompson, Mark L. *Queen of the Lakes.* Detroit, Michigan: Wayne State University Press, 1994.

Wenstadt, Tom. Freighters of Manitowoc. Bloomington, Indiana: Authorhouse, 2007.

Wolf, Julius F., Jr. *Lake Superior Shipwrecks.* Duluth, Minnesota: Lake Superior Port Cities, Inc., 1990.

Wright, Richard J. *Freshwater Whales.* Kent, Ohio: Kent State University Press, 1969.

INDEX

Vessel Index